At David C Cook, we equip the local church around the corner and around the globe to make disciples. Come see how we are working together—go to **www.davidccook.org**. Thank you!

DAVID **C** COOK™

transforming lives together

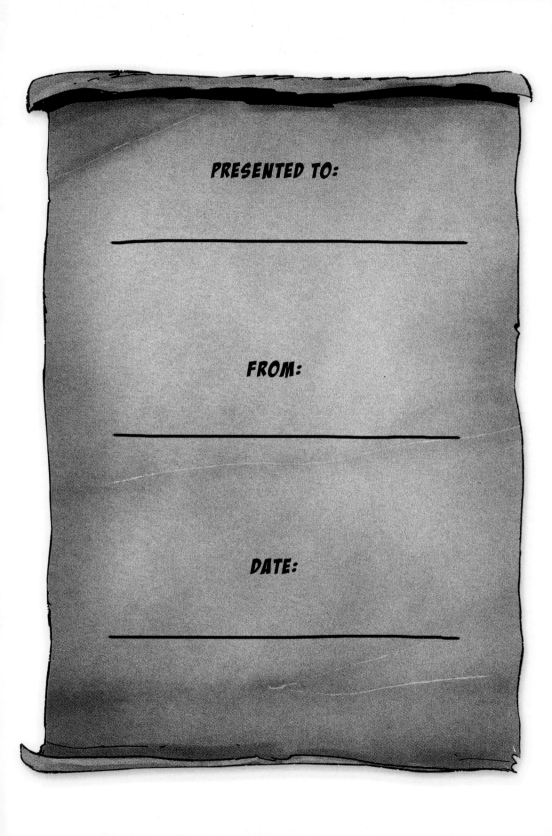

PRESENTED TO:

_____

FROM:

_____

DATE:

_____

THE ACTION BIBLE
ANYTIME DEVOTIONS

90 WAYS TO HELP KIDS CONNECT WITH GOD ANYTIME, ANYWHERE

DAVID C COOK

transforming lives together

THE ACTION BIBLE® ANYTIME DEVOTIONS
Published by David C Cook
4050 Lee Vance Drive
Colorado Springs, CO 80918 U.S.A.

Integrity Music Limited, a Division of David C Cook
Brighton, East Sussex BN1 2RE, England

The graphic circle C logo is a registered trademark of David C Cook.

All Scripture quotations are taken from THE HOLY BIBLE, NEW
INTERNATIONAL VERSION®, NIV® Copyright © 1973, 1978, 1984, 2011
by Biblica, Inc.® Used by permission. All rights reserved worldwide.

Library of Congress Control Number 2019950711
ISBN 978-0-8307-7898-0
eISBN 978-0-8307-7899-7

The Team: Stephanie Bennett, Nick Bannister, Leigh Davidson,
Rachael Stevenson, Susan Murdock
Cover Design: James Hershberger
Illustrations: Sergio Cariello

Printed in the United States of America
First Edition 2020

1 2 3 4 5 6 7 8 9 10

103119

CONTENTS

TO PARENTS & HOW TO USE

TO PARENTS

You hold in your hands a carefully collected group of devotions that invites your family to embark on an action-filled exploration of the Bible. This collection of devotions seeks to connect you and your children with the timeless Word of God through stories. Explore who God is, discover His love for each of you, and get to know Him.

EVERYONE!

These devotions and colorful illustrations will engage each child in your family—from the youngest listeners who will point to the pictures to the older readers who will devour each one on their own. Once you start exploring, you and your family will have a starting point for conversations to share that will deepen your faith and love for our Creator. We've included real-world struggles that families face. Take time to talk about and wrestle with these issues.

ANYTIME!

Kids deal with topics like anger, honesty, and identity throughout the day. These devotions are written so kids can connect with God by exploring Bible truth anytime—in the morning, at bedtime, during meals, even in the car!

Whether you sit down to explore this collection together, or your time with these stories is ongoing and informal, may your children grow to know God and the value of His Word in their lives. May they love Jesus and desire to follow Him with the way they live.

YOU ARE MY REFUGE AND MY SHIELD; I HAVE PUT MY HOPE IN YOUR WORD.

PSALM 119:114

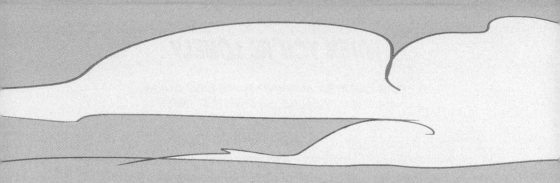

HOW TO USE FOR KIDS

What can you do when you are confronted with real-world problems? Explore God's Word! Each time you dive into these devotions, we pray that you know God better and feel closer to Him. God's Word will equip you to face your struggles, knowing that He loves you.

These devotions build a bridge to connect your world today to the wisdom of God's Word. Discover who God is and how He will grow your faith. You can be confident that He is always with you.

Every devotion sets the scene with power-packed images and then helps you:

- **Learn** God's Word with an action verse
- **Apply** it to what's happening in your life
- **Relate** it to real people from the Bible
- **Think** about it to help you grow
- **Talk** to God using quick prayer guides
- **Share** with others through questions and simple action
- **Take** it further by going back to the Bible

Enjoy your anytime time with God!

WHEN YOU'RE LONELY

*SO GOD CREATED MANKIND IN HIS OWN IMAGE ...
MALE AND FEMALE HE CREATED THEM.*

GENESIS 1:27

Do you ever feel lonely? Sometimes—even with family, friends, or a pet with you—you may have days when you feel all alone. Everyone feels like that sometimes. You might not get invited to a party, you might be left out of a game, or maybe you come across a group photo and realize no one invited you. That feeling stinks, right?

Here's something to think about: the very first words of the Bible are, "In the beginning God created ..." (Genesis 1:1). After God created light, the sky, the earth, and all the amazing animals, He created a man and a woman. The best part is that God created these people in His image, which means He created them to be like Him.

God was thoughtful in all He created, but people are very special. *You* are very special. God loves you!

Those first two people God created were named Adam and Eve, and God provided them with everything they would ever need. God loved them so much He spent time with them in the beautiful garden He made for them. And even after they messed up, God still took care of them.

When you're feeling alone, remember that God is close to you, just like He was close to Adam and Eve in the garden.

BOY JESUS
IN TEMPLE

- God created you to be exactly who you are, and He loves you very much. Tell God how you are feeling. He loves to hear from you!

- There are many ways to pray. Greet God and tell Him how your day is going. HI, GOD! SO FAR, MY DAY IS .... He wants to hear it all: your worries, joys, fears, and thanks. Open a Bible and read some verses as a prayer. Psalms is a great book of the Bible for this. You may know a familiar prayer like the Lord's Prayer. Do you know that people all around the world know and say some of the same prayers? When you pray like this, remember that you are not alone.

- In the next week, notice others who might be feeling lonely. If you get a chance, talk with them. Let them know God made you, He wants to be with you, and He helps you when you're feeling lonely. If you can't speak with them, pray for them and ask God to bring them comfort.

TAKE IT FURTHER

You can read about the story of creation in "In the Beginning" in *The Action Bible.* Or read about someone who felt lonely in Psalm 25:16–17. Even though David was a king, he still felt lonely and sad sometimes and wrote many songs and poems to God about his feelings.

JOSEPH & BROTHERS

ADAM & EVE

WHEN YOU FEEL LIKE HIDING

THEN THE MAN AND HIS WIFE HEARD THE SOUND OF THE LORD GOD AS HE WAS WALKING IN THE GARDEN IN THE COOL OF THE DAY, AND THEY HID FROM THE LORD GOD AMONG THE TREES OF THE GARDEN. BUT THE LORD GOD CALLED TO THE MAN, "WHERE ARE YOU?"

GENESIS 3:8–9

Before Emma's parents left for the night, they reminded Emma to do what the sitter, Maria, said, but she wasn't any fun. When Emma asked if they could cook something together, Maria said no. Emma knew how to turn on the stove, but she didn't realize a kitchen towel was touching the burner and a small fire started. Maria put out the fire quickly. Emma couldn't believe what had almost happened and ran to her room. When Emma's parents came home, she was scared to face them. They came to her room and talked with her about the importance of obeying. They loved Emma so much. It was hard, but she apologized to Maria for not listening to her.

Like Emma wanted to hide from her parents, Adam and Eve hid from God in the garden. God gave them one important instruction: don't eat from the tree in the middle of the garden. A serpent told Eve it would be okay, so she did. Adam did too. They disobeyed God and when they heard Him coming, they tried to hide.

In His great love for them, God had to send them away from the garden. But He had a plan to bring them back.

NAAMAN &
SERVANT GIRL

- We all do things that are wrong. What we choose to do when we make bad choices is important. It may seem easy to hide, but you will always be found. When your parents discipline you, it's because they love you and want you to learn so you won't make the same choices again. God loves you even more!

- Finish this prayer quietly to yourself: FATHER GOD, I KNOW I MAKE BAD CHOICES SOMETIMES. HELP ME REMEMBER THAT I NEVER NEED TO HIDE FROM YOU. YOU WILL ALWAYS LOVE ME. THESE ARE SOME BAD CHOICES I HAVE MADE ... HELP ME TO OBEY YOU.

- Do you have a story like Emma's? Share it or the story of Adam and Eve in the garden with someone. Answer these questions together: Have you ever felt like hiding after making a bad choice? How did it work out? What can you do besides hide? How can you help someone who might feel like she needs to hide? How can you encourage her using Adam and Eve's story?

TAKE IT FURTHER

You can read about Adam and Eve in the garden and God's loving response in "Tempted in the Garden" in *The Action Bible*. Read Hebrews 4:13–16 to discover more about how God is with us and the relief in knowing that nothing is truly hidden from Him.

JESUS & BLIND MAN

NOAH & ANIMALS

WHEN HOPE IS HARD TO SEE

"YOU ARE THE GOD WHO SEES ME," FOR SHE SAID,
"I HAVE NOW SEEN THE ONE WHO SEES ME."

GENESIS 16:13

Jocelyn was feeling down again. Her friends excitedly chatted over lunch about their plans for the upcoming holiday. She knew she should be happy too, but she just couldn't shake this sadness she felt since her grandma died a few weeks ago.

Her friends wanted to help. They wanted her to be happy again! But only her mom and dad understood and told her that these feelings of sadness were normal. Jocelyn hoped she would feel better … but when?

In the Bible, Hagar was someone who was short on hope. She was being mistreated so she ran away. She couldn't see any way out! But God sent an angel to remind her that she was important to Him. Hagar listened and knew that God noticed her in her time of sadness. God had seen her fears and worries. God gave Hagar hope because she realized that He saw her and was looking after her.

JOSHUA & WALL OF JERICHO

PRODIGAL SON & FATHER

Here are some things that might help when you're feeling sad:

- Talk about your feelings with your parents or a trusted friend. Sometimes sadness can stay with us a long time. Some people get angry when they are sad or just feel numb—like they don't want to do anything. Long-lasting sadness can be something called depression. It's important to talk to an adult if you have sadness that you just can't move past.

- Close your eyes and think about three things that make you happy, or that you are thankful for. Focusing on being grateful is a way to feel better when you are sad.

- Talk to God. Here's one idea for how to do that: GOD, I'M SO GLAD YOU ARE ALWAYS WITH ME. IT GIVES ME HOPE TO KNOW THAT THROUGH YOU SADNESS CAN END. THANK YOU FOR ALWAYS LISTENING TO ME. I LOVE YOU! AMEN.

- A dove is a bird that represents hope. Find a family member or a friend and go outside. Sit in a comfortable place or lay down in the grass and watch for birds. While you're watching, talk about things that make you happy or hopeful.

TAKE IT FURTHER

Read the story of Hagar in "Insufficient Sons" in *The Action Bible*. Read Genesis 8 to learn more about how the dove is a symbol of hope and Romans 15:13 for some encouragement when you are feeling sad.

ABRAHAM, SARAH, & ISAAC

WHEN YOU NEED TO LISTEN

"I AM SENDING YOU TO PHARAOH TO BRING MY PEOPLE
THE ISRAELITES OUT OF EGYPT." BUT MOSES SAID TO GOD,
"WHO AM I ...?" AND GOD SAID, "I WILL BE WITH YOU."

EXODUS 3:10-12

What was Coach thinking, Carver wondered, putting him in to sub as goalie when there were better players available? This was his first season playing, and he had barely practiced this position! Stace and Axle, his teammates, were staring at him from the sidelines. This was going to be ugly!

Have you ever been asked to do something, and you didn't think you were the right person? It might have felt frightening, but you looked to your coach or parents and trusted they knew best. There's someone in the Bible who was in the same position: Moses. Think for a moment about how Moses may have felt.

One day Moses was taking care of the flock of sheep that belonged to his father-in-law, Jethro. Suddenly, a bush burst into flames, and through the fire God spoke to Moses. God had seen how His people, the Israelites, were abused, and He wanted Moses to go to Pharaoh and then lead His people out of Egypt. Moses wondered why him? He asked God many questions. God answered them all. Moses listened and trusted because God said He would be with Moses.

SAMSON & DELILAH

JESUS &
HEALED WOMAN

22

In the same way, you can ask God any question about anything. God always listens and promises to be with you.

- Spend time with God, talking and listening to Him. Reading His Word and talking to a trusted adult are ways to work through things you have questions about. God might even use that person to answer your prayers.

- Here's a way you can pray: FATHER GOD, HELP ME TRUST AND KNOW THAT YOU WILL ANSWER MY PRAYERS. PLEASE BE WITH ME AS I LISTEN FOR YOUR ANSWERS. HELP ME HEAR YOU THROUGHOUT THE DAY. AMEN.

- Think about a family member, teammate, or friend who might need some encouraging words to get through something hard, like working on a new skill or dealing with an illness. Write the person a note to let him know that God is with him, and he can trust God by talking to Him through prayer. Offer to pray with this person too!

TAKE IT FURTHER

You can find the story of Moses leading the Israelites in "20,000 Egyptians Under the Sea" in *The Action Bible*. Exodus 13:17—14:31 tells the exciting story of Moses taking God's people away from Pharaoh's rule and out of Egypt.

MOSES & RED SEA

23

FOR IMPOSSIBLE TIMES

"WATCH ME," HE TOLD THEM. "FOLLOW MY LEAD. WHEN I GET TO THE EDGE OF THE CAMP, DO EXACTLY AS I DO. WHEN I AND ALL WHO ARE WITH ME BLOW OUR TRUMPETS, THEN FROM ALL AROUND THE CAMP BLOW YOURS AND SHOUT, 'FOR THE LORD AND FOR GIDEON.'"

JUDGES 7:17–18

Kara couldn't believe what was happening. Her favorite teacher just accused her of cheating on the science test. Kara was crushed! Now she was being sent to the office to talk to the principal. How would she explain what happened? Could she convince them to let her retake the test to prove she knew the material? Would she ever regain her teacher's trust?

Has anything in your life ever seemed impossible? How did you overcome it?

Gideon did not feel at all like a great warrior when God sent him to fight against His people's enemies, the Midianites. Before the battle, God spoke to Gideon and told him he had too many soldiers. Too many sounds just right! But God gave Gideon specific instructions to send certain soldiers home and, although Gideon has started with 32,000 men, he ended with only 300. Gideon was nervous, but God encouraged him. Just as God told them to do, the army surrounded Midian and blew trumpets—all at the same time. The Midianites panicked and fled or turned on one another.

Gideon and his soldiers won a battle that seemed impossible. Gideon trusted and courageously listened to God in the midst of an overwhelming conflict.

PAUL & BLINDING LIGHT

DEBORAH & BARAK

God still talks to His people—to us—and gives courage.

- To have courage means to be brave, to do a good thing that you might not be fully comfortable doing. When you are in a conflict, an argument, or a disagreement, remember that God will give you courage when you ask for it, but He wants you to turn to Him.

- Remember: you can pray out loud or quietly. You can pray anywhere, and God will hear you. Open your day with a prayer: GOOD MORNING, GOD! TODAY IS GOING TO BE HARD FOR ME. I HAVE TO TALK TO .... WILL YOU HELP ME REMEMBER THAT YOU'RE WITH ME AND GIVE ME THE RIGHT WORDS TO SAY? PLEASE HELP ME TO BE BRAVE. AMEN.

- Do you need God's help today? List the things that are on your mind. Maybe you have problems with a friend, your sibling, or a parent. As you write, ask God for courage to face each issue. Save the list. Go back later and write down how God helped you.

TAKE IT FURTHER

You can find the story of Gideon going to battle in "Cowardly Judge" in *The Action Bible*. Dealing with conflict is rarely easy. Look up the following verses for some encouragement: 1 Corinthians 16:13 and Deuteronomy 31:6.

RAHAB & ISRAELITE SCOUTS

FOR SHOWING GOD'S LOVE

BUT RUTH REPLIED, "DON'T URGE ME TO LEAVE YOU OR TO TURN BACK FROM YOU. WHERE YOU GO I WILL GO, AND WHERE YOU STAY I WILL STAY. YOUR PEOPLE WILL BE MY PEOPLE AND YOUR GOD MY GOD. WHERE YOU DIE I WILL DIE, AND THERE I WILL BE BURIED. MAY THE LORD DEAL WITH ME, BE IT EVER SO SEVERELY, IF EVEN DEATH SEPARATES YOU AND ME."

RUTH 1:16–17

Milo's stomach hurt, and he felt like he might cry. His parents had just told him that his dad had been offered a good job in a different city, and now their family was facing a big decision. They had a week to decide if they would turn down the job or face an adventure in an unfamiliar place. It would be great for his dad, but what about Milo and his brother? They liked it here.

Have you ever faced a choice that was hard for you but helped someone else? Sometimes, we make difficult choices out of love for someone else.

Naomi and her daughters-in-law faced a similar dilemma. When Naomi's husband and two sons died, she and her two daughters-in-law, Orpah and Ruth, were all alone. Naomi told the two women to leave her, to go back to their homelands, and to marry again. The women did not want to leave Naomi. She insisted, and Orpah returned home to her family, but Ruth felt a deep loyalty to

PHARAOH

PAUL'S SHIPWRECK

her mother-in-law and stayed. Together, they returned to Bethlehem where Ruth married again and where Naomi was cared for.

- Because she loved her deeply, Ruth was loyal to Naomi and stayed by her side. As a widow, Naomi had no one to care for her. What does loyalty mean to you? What would you do for the people you love?

- Close your eyes and think about your family. Thank God specifically for each person and ask Him to bless each one today. The blessing might sound like this: FATHER GOD, MAY YOU WATCH OVER AND GUIDE … TODAY. BLESS HER ACTIONS AND HELP HER BE CLOSER TO YOU.

- Are there people in your community or neighborhood who are alone? How can you show them God's love? You and your family might want to volunteer with a local organization to show God's love to the lonely.

TAKE IT FURTHER

You can read about Naomi and Ruth in "Ruth's Redeemer" in *The Action Bible*. Read Hebrews 10:24 and 1 Peter 3:8 for more about loving and caring for others.

BOAZ & RUTH
IN FIELD

WHEN THERE'S A BULLY

Amalie raced down the hall. She had prepared for the spring musical auditions for weeks. After nervously waiting, it was her turn. She stepped onto the stage, took a deep breath, and sang her first notes. However, a huddle of girls who didn't like Amalie sat in the back of the auditorium through her entire song, laughing and pointing at her. Amalie tried to finish strong, but her confidence was destroyed. Why did those mean girls have to show up? Any hope for a part in the musical was gone.

Bullies are nothing new. Thousands of years ago, a woman named Hannah knew what it was like to be bullied. Hannah loved her husband and wanted to start a family, but a long time went by and they still didn't have children. Another woman enjoyed tormenting Hannah until she cried. Hannah prayed to God at the temple. The priest saw her and thought she was drunk! Hannah explained the reason for her grief. She said that if God blessed her with a son she would dedicate his life to the church. God heard her prayers, and she had a son, Samuel.

God listens to your prayers and He is near. Remember to turn to God for help in situations that might seem hopeless.

Have you ever been teased or bullied? Or have you bullied someone else? Think about these ways of helping when bullying is going on:

DANIEL & LIONS

MARY, JOSEPH, & BABY JESUS

- Consider simply walking up to a friend who is being treated badly and standing next to her to offer support. Your parents, a teacher, or a trusted adult can help to stop a bully. As you walk into any situation, pray for God's guidance.

- If you are the one caught up in bullying or teasing someone else (even your pesky little brother or sister!), stop and think about what you are doing. Turn the scene around. How would you feel if you were being treated like that? Ask God to help you stop.

- Pray this prayer: GOD, IT NEVER FEELS GOOD TO BE TEASED, MADE FUN OF, OR BULLIED. PLEASE GIVE ME HOPE LIKE HANNAH. HELP ME TO FEEL YOU NEAR. IF I SEE SOMEONE BEING BULLIED, GIVE ME THE STRENGTH AND COURAGE TO HELP. LORD, FORGIVE ME FOR THE TIMES I MAY HAVE HURT SOMEONE ELSE. AMEN.

- Write a short note, just three to four lines, that would give hope to someone who might be experiencing bullying.

TAKE IT FURTHER

The story of Hannah can be read in "Wake-Up Call" in *The Action Bible*. The book of Psalms was written to encourage readers and praise God. Read Psalms 25 and 33 for examples of hope.

FOR LEARNING TO PRAY

YOU, LORD, ARE FORGIVING AND GOOD, ABOUNDING IN LOVE TO ALL WHO CALL TO YOU. HEAR MY PRAYER, LORD; LISTEN TO MY CRY FOR MERCY. WHEN I AM IN DISTRESS, I CALL TO YOU, BECAUSE YOU ANSWER ME.

PSALM 86:5-7

Clark couldn't wait to visit his grandmother for the weekend. Her cozy house had always been his favorite place to go, and she had taught him so much about the Bible and Jesus. As Clark talked about some things going on with his friends, he shared that he wanted to pray for them but didn't feel like he knew how. His grandma poured him a glass of milk and sat down next to him. She assured Clark that there are no wrong ways to pray; God just wants to hear from you. The most important thing to know is that God wants you to trust Him with your concerns and to remember that He is near. We shouldn't try to do things on our own. God wants to hear it all!

Here are some ways to get started talking to God, and then you can say absolutely anything to Him:

- FATHER GOD, YOU ARE ...

- GOD, I NEED ...

- JESUS, HELP ...

- FATHER, HEAL ...

- DEAR GOD, LISTEN TO WHAT HAPPENED TODAY ...

- GOD, THANK YOU FOR ...

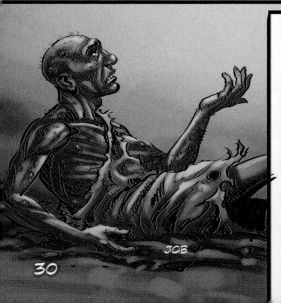

JOB

DISCIPLES IN STORM

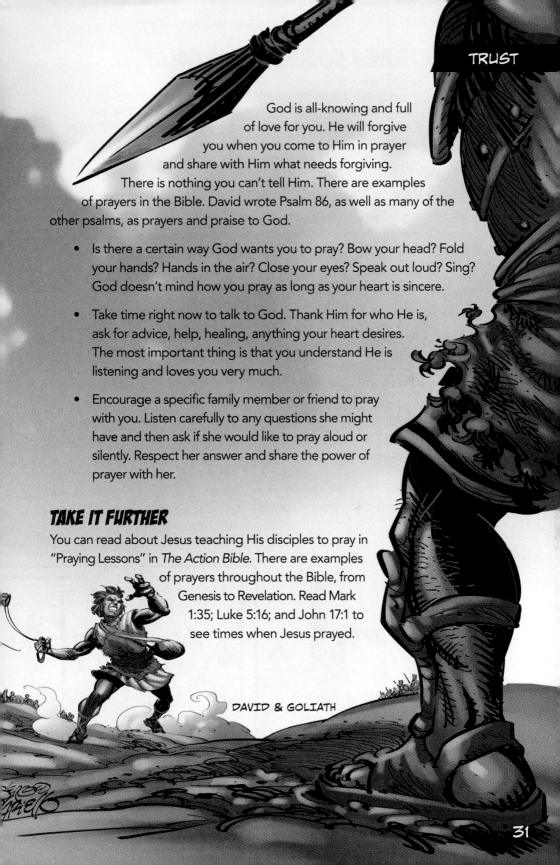

God is all-knowing and full of love for you. He will forgive you when you come to Him in prayer and share with Him what needs forgiving. There is nothing you can't tell Him. There are examples of prayers in the Bible. David wrote Psalm 86, as well as many of the other psalms, as prayers and praise to God.

- Is there a certain way God wants you to pray? Bow your head? Fold your hands? Hands in the air? Close your eyes? Speak out loud? Sing? God doesn't mind how you pray as long as your heart is sincere.

- Take time right now to talk to God. Thank Him for who He is, ask for advice, help, healing, anything your heart desires. The most important thing is that you understand He is listening and loves you very much.

- Encourage a specific family member or friend to pray with you. Listen carefully to any questions she might have and then ask if she would like to pray aloud or silently. Respect her answer and share the power of prayer with her.

TAKE IT FURTHER

You can read about Jesus teaching His disciples to pray in "Praying Lessons" in *The Action Bible*. There are examples of prayers throughout the Bible, from Genesis to Revelation. Read Mark 1:35; Luke 5:16; and John 17:1 to see times when Jesus prayed.

DAVID & GOLIATH

WHEN SOCIAL MEDIA CALLS

FOR YOU CREATED MY INMOST BEING; YOU KNIT ME TOGETHER IN MY MOTHER'S WOMB. I PRAISE YOU BECAUSE I AM FEARFULLY AND WONDERFULLY MADE; YOUR WORKS ARE WONDERFUL, I KNOW THAT FULL WELL.

PSALM 139:13-14

Alden's big sister, Kinsley, used to hang out with him and play video games. But now it seemed like all she had eyes for was social media. Keeping up with her threads of conversations and posting more and more (and more!) selfies consumed all her time. Today she had complained about how much homework she had to do when Alden asked her to play his new game, but then she wanted to check her likes. "It will only take a sec," she said. But half an hour later, she was still posting and scrolling.

Alden sighed. *Whatever,* he thought. *I'll just play with my friends online. They are much cooler anyway.*

What do you think about online stuff? Are you careful with how much time you spend on playing games or watching videos or chatting with "friends" (who could be people you've never actually met)? Is God honored by what you say and do online? Does being online ever keep you from being with real live people? Or from being with God?

God created you and loves you. He knew you before you were even born. You are wonderfully made to honor God and yourself. Think through what that means:

ANGEL & MARY

MIRIAM

- Take a look at your favorite online activities; or if you aren't online, think about what you've seen others do. Do you think about God as you're spending time online? Do your parents know about what you look at and how much time you spend online? Think of them as your protectors. You are their child, created by a loving Father God who wants the very best for you.

- You could pray like this: GOD, YOU CREATED ME AND I WANT TO HONOR YOU WITH MY ACTIONS. HELP ME MAKE SMART CHOICES AND FORGIVE ME FOR MISTAKES I HAVE MADE. WHEN I FORGET THAT I AM YOURS, GIVE ME A GENTLE REMINDER TO HELP ME KNOW THAT I AM YOUR WONDERFUL WORK. AMEN.

- Keep building up others and honoring your Father God. Ask a trusted adult to help you if you're involved with anything that you want to get out of or if you're uncomfortable with anything you've seen or read. And remember that spending time with real people is way more important than anything on a screen!

TAKE IT FURTHER

Read the story of a servant girl who honored God in the work she did in "A Miracle for a Rash" in *The Action Bible*. Exodus 20:12; Deuteronomy 5:16; Matthew 19:19; and Ephesians 6:2 are all verses that remind us to honor and respect our parents.

ESTHER & KING XERXES

ON THOSE DAYS YOU NEED TRUST

LET THE MORNING BRING ME WORD OF YOUR UNFAILING LOVE, FOR I HAVE PUT MY TRUST IN YOU. SHOW ME THE WAY I SHOULD GO, FOR TO YOU I ENTRUST MY LIFE.

PSALM 143:8

Alex dreaded mornings. As his mom had told him on multiple occasions, he was not a morning person. He knew he should be more responsible in the morning—not requiring his mom or dad to check on him to get out of bed—but he just couldn't muster any energy when his alarm went off. After hitting the snooze button multiple times, he was in no shape to begin his day with thoughts of inviting God into it.

Regardless of how you rise and greet your day, think about how you include God in your morning. God is always with you, even when you sleep. Each day is a new opportunity to learn from Him and to share His love with others. David wrote many psalms, or songs, of praise to God. In Psalm 143, David asked God to bring His love and guidance to him each morning because he trusted that God was with him.

DISCIPLES

JONATHAN

- How do you start your day? Consider a reset. Before you even open your eyes, thank God for the gift of a new day. Know that God hears you and trust that He is always listening. Share with Him things about your coming day you are both excited for and nervous about. Ask God to help you feel the presence of the Holy Spirit. Then check in with Him throughout your day and let Him know how things are going and where you might need more encouragement. Eventually, you will form a habit that will deepen your trust in God and make your relationship with Him strong.

- In the morning: GOOD MORNING GOD! THANK YOU FOR ... BE WITH ME TODAY WHEN ...
  During the day: HI, GOD! I WANTED TO CHECK IN AND TELL YOU ...
  At bedtime: FATHER GOD, TODAY WAS ... THANK YOU FOR ...
  BLESS MY DREAMS. AMEN.

- After a few days, seek out some family members or friends and share with them what you have been doing. Ask them how they start their morning. Invite them to try your new prayers and share how you start your prayers to encourage them.

TAKE IT FURTHER

You can find the story of two women, Jochebed and her daughter Miriam, who fully trusted God in "Baby in a Basket" in *The Action Bible* or read Exodus 2:1–8 to learn more.

MARY, JOSEPH, & JESUS TO EGYPT

WHEN YOU NEED REAL FRIENDS

ABOVE ALL ELSE, GUARD YOUR HEART, FOR EVERYTHING YOU DO FLOWS FROM IT.

PROVERBS 4:23

She checked again, but Cora wasn't replying. Jessica thought they were friends but when she needed her most, where was Cora? Why had she told her those secrets? Jessica's mom had cautioned her against placing too much importance on her online friends. She had told her to guard her heart and not reveal too much to someone she had never met in person. Why had she let her close friends from youth group slip away? Would she be able to restore those relationships?

The book of Proverbs is a source of guidance and wisdom for young people. The verse above states that your heart is your source of life so you should protect it. Look closely at your relationships or friendships you've allowed into your heart. They form in a variety of ways: at school, at church, on teams, in clubs or activities, or through current friends. A true friend is someone who knows and accepts you for exactly who God created you to be. Is anyone hurting you or not treating you well? Can someone you've only met online really know you? How you conduct your relationships reflects your character.

ZACCHAEUS & JESUS

KING DAVID & ABIGAIL

Jesus had very close, trustworthy friends. His disciples were His friends and He knew them by spending time with them.

- It might feel great to have a lot of attention on social media, but don't confuse any likes you receive—or don't receive—with actual friends. God wants you to guard your heart and protect yourself from relationships that might not be true friendships. If a person is making you feel bad about yourself, then that person is not your actual friend. Think of the true friendships Jesus had.

- God understands, so talk to Him: DEAR GOD, HELP ME TO SEE WHO MY TRUE FRIENDS ARE, THE ONES I DO NOT NEED TO GUARD MY HEART AGAINST. I WANT TO BE A FRIEND TO OTHERS. AMEN.

- Write down the names of three people you consider to be your closest, truest friends. List the reasons why each is such a good friend. What do you like about them? Are they trustworthy? Is your character stronger because of them? Then share with each friend why they are important to you and invest time in those positive relationships.

TAKE IT FURTHER

You can read about Jesus and His disciples in "Calling the Twelve" in *The Action Bible*. Read Luke 5:1–11; Matthew 9:9–13; and John 21:1–14 to learn more about Jesus and His friendships with the disciples.

JOHN THE BAPTIST & JESUS

BUT BLESSED IS THE ONE WHO TRUSTS IN THE LORD, WHOSE CONFIDENCE IS IN HIM. THEY WILL BE LIKE A TREE PLANTED BY THE WATER THAT SENDS OUT ITS ROOTS BY THE STREAM. IT DOES NOT FEAR WHEN THE HEAT COMES; ITS LEAVES ARE ALWAYS GREEN.

JEREMIAH 17:7-8

Jeremy couldn't believe it. It seemed like nothing was going well for him. In the last few days, he had failed a major test, cracked the screen on his tablet, gotten into a fight with his best friend, and now his parents were making him go visit his family out of town all weekend. What else could go wrong? It seemed like the pressures were mounting, and he was mad at everyone! He didn't know who to talk to.

God teaches you His truth as you spend time reading the Bible and talking to Him. When you are close to God, your source of strength, you will grow and be spiritually healthy. The verse above talks about a tree that's planted close to water. It doesn't need to fear when the sun beats down on it because the water—its constant source of nourishment—keeps it fresh and alive. When Jesus was on earth, He impacted the lives of everyone He encountered. People longed to be near Him and learn from Him because He refreshed them like water.

JACOB & ISAAC

TIMOTHY

When you are intentional about being close to God, your "roots" will be firm in Him when challenging times come.

- You can get and stay close to God in a variety of ways. Reading His Word, praying, worshipping, and praising God are some examples. Can you think of others? Life can be hard and surprises will come your way, so be prepared by trusting God and planting yourself firmly in His presence.

- Pray this prayer: LOVING GOD, I TRUST YOU ALWAYS. HELP ME TO GROW MY ROOTS CLOSE TO YOU SO YOUR SPIRIT CAN ALWAYS FEED ME. HELP ME BE AN EXAMPLE TO OTHERS OF WHAT IT MEANS TO TRUST YOU. AMEN.

- What distracts you from God? If you feel yourself drifting from Him, intentionally get back in His presence. How can you praise Him at home, at school, at practice, or in the car?

TAKE IT FURTHER

Find the story of the prophet Jeremiah in "Unpopular Prophesies" in *The Action Bible* or read John 2:1–9 and Jeremiah 23:1–12.

SAMARITAN WOMAN
& JESUS

I WAITED PATIENTLY FOR THE LORD; HE TURNED TO ME AND HEARD MY CRY.

PSALM 40:1

One day, Isabel and Max's dad came home from work and shared some bad news: he had lost his job. Because their family had faith in God, every morning Isabel's family prayed together and took turns leading. The first morning after the news, Isabel's mom asked God to bring their family closer together with this challenge. The next day, her dad prayed that God would provide a new job for him. Isabel was nervous and asked not to lead. A couple of weeks went by and every day the family continued to pray together. Isabel passed but took comfort in her family gathering and giving their problems to God.

One morning, Isabel felt differently, even a little excited, as the family gathered for their prayer time. She felt it was important to lead for her family that day. "God, I am a little bit nervous here. We all love You very much and we trust You. We know You will take care of us. We believe in You. We have faith. Amen." Isabel's parents were glad to have her praying with them. The family faithfully continued talking with God every day, and God answered their prayers.

In the Bible, we hear how David defeated the giant Goliath because he trusted that God's power was greater than anything else. David knew at a young age God had chosen him to be king but it took many years and a whole lot of running for his life before David entered his kingly role. He spent much of that time

ESAU

LEAH & RACHEL

talking honestly to God and asking for help. You can find many of his prayers and songs to God in the book of Psalms.

- Faith in God requires trust. Similar to how we know the wind exists but we can't see it directly, God is near and working in your life. Your faith will increase by studying the Bible, sharing God's stories with others, and learning more about Him at places like church or Bible camp.

- Finish this prayer silently, AMAZING GOD, I WANT TO FEEL YOU NEAR ME. HELP ME WHEN ... BLESS THE FOLLOWING MEMBERS OF MY FAMILY ... HELP THEM TO ... AMEN.

- Invite the family members who live in your house to join you in a family prayer time, just like Isabel's family. Explain that you would like to spend time together talking to God. Be ready to lead and have faith that God will be with you during this time.

TAKE IT FURTHER

You can read one story of David's faith in "A Giant Challenge" in *The Action Bible*. Read Matthew 6:9–13 and discover a prayer written for all of God's followers to pray.

JESUS & BOY WITH LUNCH

WHEN YOU NEED A PLAN

"FOR I KNOW THE PLANS I HAVE FOR YOU," DECLARES THE LORD, "PLANS TO PROSPER YOU AND NOT TO HARM YOU, PLANS TO GIVE YOU HOPE AND A FUTURE. THEN YOU WILL CALL ON ME AND COME AND PRAY TO ME, AND I WILL LISTEN TO YOU. YOU WILL SEEK ME AND FIND ME WHEN YOU SEEK ME WITH ALL YOUR HEART."

JEREMIAH 29:11-13

What day is it? Hailey had to be sure she packed the right gear in the morning because with all her activities, she didn't want to forget what she'd need later that day. It was a little hard to keep track of everything going on. Should she drop something? She was only in fourth grade but was active in after-school clubs, scouts, volleyball, soccer, dance classes, and children's choir at church. It was fun but she often found herself getting tired and forgetting things. What did God want for her?

Jeremiah was a prophet who wrote a letter to confirm what God told Ezekiel in an incredible vision. At the time of this letter, God's people were being held captive in the city of Babylon. God wanted His people to hold tight and trust that He would provide for them. He not only had a plan for their lives, but He wanted them to come to Him in prayer and reminded them that He would listen.

JESUS, MARY, & MARTHA

JOSHUA & PROMISED LAND

God's plans for you are filled with hope and promise. It's reassuring to know God loves us and we can trust in His plans.

- Lots of activities and a full schedule can be fun—as long as they don't pull you away from time with God. Just know that God the Father already has a good and perfect plan for your life. Trust Him and ask Him what He has for you.

- When you're feeling overwhelmed: DEAR GOD, SOMETIMES IT CAN BE HARD TO SLOW DOWN MY BUSY LIFE AND TAKE TIME TO LISTEN TO WHAT YOU WANT TO TELL ME. PLEASE HELP ME TO BE AWARE OF YOUR PRESENCE IN MY LIFE. I WANT YOU TO GUIDE ME. AMEN.

- Take a walk or simply sit outside and spend intentional time with God today. Quiet your mind, take some deep breaths, and ask Him to speak to you. Listen carefully and enjoy your time. Consider inviting a family member or friend to sit in silence with you, then share how you felt God or heard from Him.

TAKE IT FURTHER

Ezekiel's vision is shown in "Ezekiel's Exile" in *The Action Bible* or the book of Ezekiel.

MARY & JESUS

JESUS & LAZARUS

TAKE TIME TO DEVELOP FRIENDSHIPS

*NOW WHEN JESUS SAW THE CROWDS, HE WENT UP
ON A MOUNTAINSIDE AND SAT DOWN. HIS DISCIPLES
CAME TO HIM, AND HE BEGAN TO TEACH THEM.*

MATTHEW 5:1-2

Mackenzie's friends were a lot of fun—always laughing—and she enjoyed being with them. But some of their choices made her nervous, such as daring one another to do stupid stuff. One night after watching a movie at the theater together, Mackenzie and her friends stayed to talk to some boys who had been causing trouble during the show. The boys made Mackenzie feel uncomfortable, but her friends seemed to like the attention. Mackenzie decided to text her dad to come pick her up.

Friends are the people you spend the most time with. They can influence you in either positive or negative ways. That's why it is important to choose like-minded friends you respect and who will be kind to you in return.

Jesus was thoughtful about the people He chose to spend time with. After praying alone on a mountain, He came down and named His twelve disciples. These men were all close to Jesus and He respected them. Jesus' disciples weren't perfect, but He surrounded Himself with men who would make a difference in the world.

JESUS &
DISCIPLES

JESUS ON
DONKEY

- It's not always easy to develop and grow true friendships. It may take time and effort to find positive people. God created you and has a plan for you. Be your true self and know that should be enough for people you consider to be friends. You can respect and honor God by being thoughtful with the friendships you pursue and the people you surround yourself with.

- You can talk to God anytime: GOD, YOU KNOW ME BEST. PLEASE GIVE ME THE WISDOM TO CHOOSE FRIENDS WHO RESPECT ME, RESPECT YOU, AND HELP ME BECOME THE BEST PERSON I CAN BE. THANK YOU FOR LOVING ME SO MUCH THAT YOU WANT THE VERY BEST FRIENDS FOR ME. AMEN.

- Think about your current friends. Why do you like them? What do you like to do together? Are they positive people who encourage you? What kinds of choices do your friends influence you to make? How do they help you to grow closer to God?

TAKE IT FURTHER

Read about Jesus selecting His disciples in "Sermon on a Mountain" in *The Action Bible*. Matthew 5–7 contains the full message Jesus shared with the crowd after naming His disciples.

JEZEBEL & ELIJAH

PETER & JESUS

ALWAYS TIME TO FORGIVE

THEN PETER CAME TO JESUS AND ASKED, "LORD, HOW MANY TIMES SHALL I FORGIVE MY BROTHER OR SISTER WHO SINS AGAINST ME? UP TO SEVEN TIMES?" JESUS ANSWERED, "I TELL YOU, NOT SEVEN TIMES, BUT SEVENTY-SEVEN TIMES."

MATTHEW 18:21-22

Sarah and David are sister and brother and spend a lot of time together—especially in the summer. They enjoy trying to beat each other in their video games. One day David was playing his highest-scoring game ever. Sarah was ready for her turn and growing impatient. Thinking it would be funny, she lazily pushed some buttons on the game, forcing David's turn to end. It worked, but David lost his high score. He was so mad he screamed at Sarah and chased her to her room where she slammed the door in his face. That was it! David was never playing with her again!

When someone wrongs you, it can be very hard to forgive that person, let alone show love to him or her. Doesn't it feel better to yell or turn a cold shoulder? Let's face it, we all do rotten things sometimes. Friends can be insensitive. Siblings can be the worst.

When Jesus was teaching and Peter asked him how many times we have to forgive a person, His response surprised everyone. There really is no forgiveness limit. Would you want there to be a limit for you?

SAUL & SAMUEL

ANGEL & JACOB

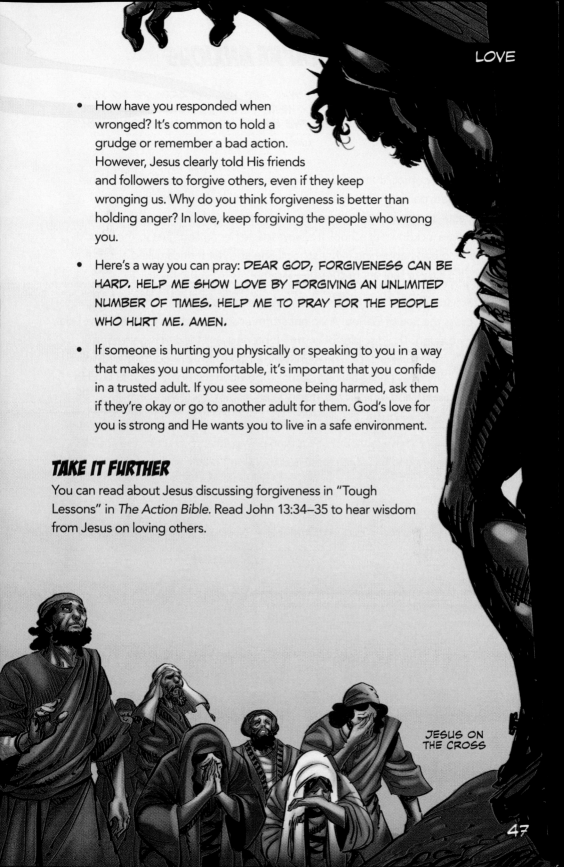

- How have you responded when wronged? It's common to hold a grudge or remember a bad action. However, Jesus clearly told His friends and followers to forgive others, even if they keep wronging us. Why do you think forgiveness is better than holding anger? In love, keep forgiving the people who wrong you.

- Here's a way you can pray: DEAR GOD, FORGIVENESS CAN BE HARD. HELP ME SHOW LOVE BY FORGIVING AN UNLIMITED NUMBER OF TIMES. HELP ME TO PRAY FOR THE PEOPLE WHO HURT ME. AMEN.

- If someone is hurting you physically or speaking to you in a way that makes you uncomfortable, it's important that you confide in a trusted adult. If you see someone being harmed, ask them if they're okay or go to another adult for them. God's love for you is strong and He wants you to live in a safe environment.

TAKE IT FURTHER

You can read about Jesus discussing forgiveness in "Tough Lessons" in *The Action Bible*. Read John 13:34–35 to hear wisdom from Jesus on loving others.

JESUS ON THE CROSS

WHEN YOU'RE ANXIOUS

HE SAID TO HIS DISCIPLES, "WHY ARE YOU SO AFRAID? DO YOU STILL HAVE NO FAITH?" THEY WERE TERRIFIED AND ASKED EACH OTHER, "WHO IS THIS? EVEN THE WIND AND THE WAVES OBEY HIM!"

MARK 4:40-41

Maddie was getting that weird feeling again. She couldn't explain it, but she felt stressed, panicky, and afraid. It started when she heard the forecast at breakfast—more storms were on the way with possible flooding. Then they practiced a lockdown at school. It always made her anxious just to think about something bad happening in her school! She and her friends talked about it at lunch. It's easy to feel out of control—like that storm in the Bible.

After a long day of teaching crowds, Jesus and His disciples boarded a boat to cross the Sea of Galilee. A violent storm erupted and waves tossed the boat around. The disciples became frightened and tried to regain control while Jesus slept. The men were afraid they were going to drown! Without saying a word, Jesus stood up in the boat, reached out His hand, and quieted the storm. In an instant, there was calm.

In times of turmoil, it can be hard to remember that Jesus is with you— to remember to have faith. But Jesus is all-powerful and can calm the scariest things. The key is to have faith that He is there and is able to help you.

BOY JESUS
IN TEMPLE

- God is in control and has a plan for you. As your day gets busy with family demands, friend drama, tests, and practices, it might feel like a storm is brewing all around you. Jesus is with you, in your boat. Look to Him to take control. The best way to do this is to practice it. Invite Him into your life every day. The more you practice, the easier it will be to remember that He is in your boat.

- God always hears you, so tell Him: GOD, YOU ARE ALL-POWERFUL AND I AM THANKFUL! THANK YOU FOR BEING IN MY BOAT, READY TO STAND UP WHEN I AM AFRAID. PLEASE HELP ME TO REMEMBER YOU ARE CLOSE TO ME IN SCARY TIMES AND YOU CAN CALM MY STORMS. AMEN.

- Grab some paper and something to write with. Draw a simple boat, filling up most of the paper. Inside the boat, write down things that have been or are overwhelming to you. Say them out loud and pray for God to stand up and help you through the scary things.

TAKE IT FURTHER

You can read about Jesus quieting the storm in "Storm at Sea" in *The Action Bible*. Read Joshua 1:9 and Philippians 4:6 for more encouraging words.

JOSEPH & BROTHERS

ADAM & EVE

WHEN OTHERS NEED YOU

"'LOVE THE LORD YOUR GOD WITH ALL YOUR HEART AND WITH ALL YOUR SOUL AND WITH ALL YOUR STRENGTH AND WITH ALL YOUR MIND'; AND, 'LOVE YOUR NEIGHBOR AS YOURSELF.'"

LUKE 10:27

Every day on the way home, the elderly lady was there. She sat on her porch with her little dog and watched Leon and his friends as they walked home. Sometimes she smiled or nodded at the boys. Today though, her little dog wasn't with her and she had a walker next to her; she wasn't smiling. Leon noticed and mentioned it to his mother when he got home. She put together a plate of cookies and a small vase of flowers for Leon to take to her. When he stepped onto her porch and asked if she was okay, her smile returned. He would take the time to find out what had happened.

A man asked Jesus what he must do to gain eternal life. Jesus answered by telling him to love God with his whole heart and to love his neighbor as he loves himself. Jesus then told a parable or story to help the man better understand who his neighbor is. The story was about a Jewish traveler robbers attacked and left for dead on the road. Only a Samaritan man (often considered an enemy to the Jews) stopped to help the wounded man. Jesus said this Samaritan man was

NAAMAN &
SERVANT GIRL

a true neighbor. Jesus wants all His followers to do the same:
to act in love and to care for others.

- Showing love and kindness to strangers is important, but it should be done in a safe way, sometimes with adult supervision. When you believe in Jesus and follow His ways, you are His disciple. Being a disciple is a big responsibility because people look to disciples to learn what their teacher is like.

- You could pray like this: LOVING GOD, I WANT TO BE A GOOD NEIGHBOR. SHOW ME WAYS TO HELP OTHERS EACH DAY SO THEY WILL KNOW YOUR LOVE THROUGH ME. AMEN.

- Write a list of everyone you interact with on a typical day. This list might include your family members, bus driver, teachers, coach, director, neighbor, etc. Then ask yourself: How do I treat them? How can I let God's love work through me to care for them?

TAKE IT FURTHER

You can read the parable Jesus told in "A Good Neighbor" in *The Action Bible* or in Luke 10:25–37.

JESUS &
BLIND MAN

NOAH & ANIMALS

WHENEVER YOU LEAD

*"I AM THE GOOD SHEPHERD. THE GOOD SHEPHERD
LAYS DOWN HIS LIFE FOR THE SHEEP."*

JOHN 10:11

Jerod used to enjoy playing sports during recess. It didn't matter what kind of game it was, he just liked being active outside with his friends. But lately some of the bigger kids were taking charge of the games and ruining the fun. The big kids only passed to their friends, ignored the younger kids, and made up rules that didn't make sense. The teachers thought they deserved to be leaders, but they weren't acting in honorable ways.

In Bible times, Jesus wanted people to understand that He is the Son of God sent to save God's people, so He compared Himself to a shepherd. The people understood that a shepherd is a strong leader who takes excellent care of his sheep and protects his flock. The people wanted to follow Jesus.

JOSHUA & WALL
OF JERICHO

PRODIGAL SON
& FATHER

There is honor in being a strong leader like Jesus who looks out for the people He leads and doesn't use influence to control others.

- Picture an area of your life where you are a leader. Maybe you are a big brother or sister or maybe kids in your class look to you for ideas for what to do for fun. Do you think the way you lead is honoring God? You may not be asked to lay down your life for someone like a shepherd would for his sheep, but you can show love and respect for others by listening and including people equally.

- Take time to ask God: DEAR GOD, HELP ME SUPPORT THE LEADERS IN MY LIFE IN THE BEST WAY POSSIBLE. WHEN YOU WANT ME TO LEAD, HELP ME LEAD WITH STRENGTH AND HONOR. AMEN.

- Think about the leaders in your life. Who leads you at school? At recess? At church? What makes a good leader? Ask a close friend if he thinks you would be a good leader. Why or why not?

TAKE IT FURTHER
You can read the story of Jesus as the Good Shepherd in "Faith at First Sight" in *The Action Bible*. Read Psalm 23 for a famous illustration of a shepherd.

ABRAHAM, SARAH, & ISAAC

A TIME TO HELP

This wasn't the first time Ellie had seen the kid come in late to class, pushing past other students and uttering bad words under his breath. She usually tried to steer clear of Jack because if he wasn't causing trouble, he was getting into it. She was trying to calm her nerves before the huge test. The teacher began passing out the exams. Clearly Jack wasn't ready. He didn't even have a pencil. Unexpectedly, Ellie felt a sudden urge to give Jack one of her brand-new pencils. *Really, God? I'm scared of him!* She cautiously leaned toward him with a small smile and a pencil in her hand. His surprised nod and quick thanks let her know that God was with her and Jack.

After Jesus died and was resurrected, Saul searched for, imprisoned, and killed followers of Jesus. As he traveled one day, a light from heaven flashed and Jesus spoke to him. After the encounter, Saul was blind. Jesus came to a man named Ananias in a vision and told him to go to Saul and place his hands on him. God would heal Saul's sight. Ananias feared Saul and did not want to go! But he obediently listened to Jesus and went. God worked a miracle by healing Saul's

SAMSON & DELILAH

JESUS &
HEALED WOMAN

blindness through Ananias. Because these men were willing to serve, others would come to know Jesus!

- Be willing to serve others when God asks you. There are opportunities around you every day to share the love of God with people who are in need or hurting. Keep your eyes open to those around you, or the Holy Spirit may give you a nudge to specifically act. Don't ignore or talk yourself out of those instances. You may miss out on introducing someone to Jesus.

- Close your eyes and talk to God. FATHER GOD, I WANT TO BE READY TO SERVE OTHERS WHEN YOU CALL. I KNOW YOU CAN DO INCREDIBLE THINGS AND CHANGE LIVES. WORK THROUGH ME. AMEN.

- As you go about your day, instead of looking down at a device, challenge yourself to keep your eyes up to see others and look for ways to serve them. Talk with a friend or family member about ideas to show the love of Jesus.

TAKE IT FURTHER

You can experience the story of Paul in "A Blinding Light" in *The Action Bible* or read Acts 9:1–18.

MOSES & RED SEA

WHEN YOU'RE NOT SURE HOW TO SHOW LOVE

LOVE IS PATIENT, LOVE IS KIND. IT DOES NOT ENVY, IT DOES NOT BOAST, IT IS NOT PROUD. IT DOES NOT DISHONOR OTHERS, IT IS NOT SELF-SEEKING, IT IS NOT EASILY ANGERED, IT KEEPS NO RECORD OF WRONGS.... IT ALWAYS PROTECTS, ALWAYS TRUSTS, ALWAYS HOPES, ALWAYS PERSEVERES.

1 CORINTHIANS 13:4-5, 7

Ryan, Sean, and Jackie were siblings who constantly fought. What game to play? Who gets the best controller? What seat in the car? Who has to feed the dog? Everything was a battle. Nothing was decided without bickering. Many times the arguments ended in a physical wrestling match with someone getting hurt. Finally their parents decided something needed to change in their home. Their father gathered the family and they worked together to decide how they wanted to interact with one another. After talking they wrote a family mission statement to guide their actions: "We are a family full of love. We will be patient and kind with one another. Our love must be pure and build up one another up. We will hold our tempers and stop keeping score about how we are hurting one another. We will celebrate good things and stay away from the bad. Let's be a family that protects one another and places our trust and hope in the Lord."

Do those words sound familiar? Paul, one of the early leaders of the church, wrote to encourage the people of Corinth, a town that was full of fighting and bickering. The words of 1 Corinthians 13:4–7 were sent to remind them that love

PAUL & BLINDING LIGHT

DEBORAH & BARAK

is important above all. Like your parents sometimes need to step in, Paul called for the people to treat one another like God wanted.

- Out of respect and to honor God, it is important that you show love to others. Should you show love to your siblings when you feel like fighting? To your parents when they correct you? To your coach when she makes you run an extra lap? When it comes to showing love to others, the answer is always yes.

- When you're feeling thankful, pray: LOVING GOD, YOU ARE THE FATHER TO US ALL. THANK YOU FOR LOVING ME SO MUCH. PLEASE CONTINUE TO SHOW ME WAYS TO LOVE OTHERS. AMEN.

- Talk with your family about creating your own family mission statement or plan for how you want to act toward one another. Consider writing it down and displaying it in your home.

TAKE IT FURTHER

You can read about Paul's letter in "Corinthian Court" in *The Action Bible* or see 1 Corinthians 13:13 for another great verse about love.

RAHAB & ISRAELITE SCOUTS

WHEN LIVES NEED TO CHANGE

THEREFORE, IF ANYONE IS IN CHRIST, THE NEW CREATION HAS COME: THE OLD HAS GONE, THE NEW IS HERE!

2 CORINTHIANS 5:17

Grace's uncle caused a lot of stress in her family. He had trouble keeping a job and sometimes he was homeless. He abused drugs, which meant he was an addict. Addiction is a disease that often leads to other problems for the people dealing with it, as well as the people who love them. Grace's mom was always worried about her brother, and she did what she could to care for him. Things finally got so bad for Grace's uncle that he realized he wanted to change. With the support of his family, he went to a rehabilitation facility where he decided to take steps to get healthy. He became sober and started to learn that his life mattered. Most importantly, Grace's uncle was reminded about God's love for him. The old ways were gone in his life and the new was coming! Everyone has the ability to change through Christ.

Throughout the Bible, it's amazing to see how God uses ordinary people to do incredible things. Jesus once encountered a Samaritan woman at a well. She was an outcast in her community because of choices she made. Her life was hard. When she met Jesus, He told her how her life could change if she followed Him. It would be like having Living Water instead of water from a well. She would

PAUL'S SHIPWRECK

PHARAOH

never be thirsty again! She shared His good news with everyone in her village. Jesus made her life new.

- Even when things in life seem impossible, there is always hope. That hope exists because Jesus came to this earth for all people. God loves us so much that He sent His Son for our salvation. When things like addiction impact a family, things can feel hopeless. You can turn to God for renewed hope through prayer knowing He can help.

- Finish this prayer silently: FATHER GOD, PLEASE GIVE ME HOPE WHEN THINGS FEEL HOPELESS. HELP ME TO BRING YOUR HOPE TO OTHERS. ESPECIALLY ... AMEN.

- Look for verses in your Bible about God's hope through Jesus and write several encouraging notes. Share them with someone you know who is in need or ask a parent or trusted adult to share the notes with an organization or ministry that might need them.

TAKE IT FURTHER

You can read about the Samaritan woman's story in "Living Water" in *The Action Bible* or in John 4:1–42. Read Romans 6:4 for another reference to new life in Christ.

BOAZ & RUTH
IN FIELD

WHEN YOU NEED GUIDANCE

*THE FRUIT OF THE SPIRIT IS LOVE, JOY, PEACE,
FOREBEARANCE, KINDNESS, GOODNESS, FAITHFULNESS,
GENTLENESS AND SELF-CONTROL... SINCE WE LIVE BY
THE SPIRIT, LET US KEEP IN STEP WITH THE SPIRIT.*

GALATIANS 5:22-23, 25

You're not sure what's going on, but your mom is close to grounding you and your best friend keeps picking fights with everyone. Is there a place to get some clear guidance on how to manage family dynamics, school demands, friends, and social media?

The guidance for daily living Paul offered in his letter to the Galatians is just as practical for you today. He wrote letters to churches in different cities (like Galatia) to help them stay close to God. He wrote that, similar to a fruit-bearing tree, God's Spirit produces fruit in our lives when we keep in step with Him. What nine things did Paul say would show in your life when you walk with God?

LOVE: Whether people treat you nicely or meanly, the Spirit helps you respond with love.

JOY: Start each day by inviting God to bring joy to you and those you impact.

PEACE: Ask the Spirit to help you bring peace when you can. If a discussion gets heated, take a step back, think, and pray for wisdom from the Lord.

FOREBEARANCE: Also known as patience. You love your family, but it can be hard to get along. Ask the Spirit to help you be patient.

KINDNESS: It can be easy to tear down people or nit pick others' faults. Pray to be kinder to others.

GOODNESS: Ask God to show you His goodness and how to share it with others.

DANIEL & LIONS

MARY, JOSEPH, & BABY JESUS

FAITHFULNESS: Start each day with God and check in multiple times. Conclude your day by thanking Him for the good and bad that will bring you closer to Him.

GENTLENESS: Choose your words carefully and communicate with respect.

SELF-CONTROL: Ask God to help you think before you act.

- It may seem that if you just try harder you can do better. But being close to God and allowing His Spirit to shape you is actually what changes you. When you surrender your life to Him, He grows His fruit in you. Which of these areas of your life do you see God growing in you? Which areas need more growth?

- You could ask God something like this: WISE GOD, HELP ME SEE THE AREAS OF MY LIFE THAT ARE OUT OF STEP WITH YOUR SPIRIT. HELP ME WALK WITH YOU AND GROW YOUR FRUIT IN MY LIFE. AMEN.

- List the nine fruit of the Spirit and jot down your own ideas for ways to live them out with the people you know. Pray for God to lead you as you seek to live your life in this God-honoring way.

TAKE IT FURTHER

You can read about some young men who kept in step with the Spirit even when it was hard in "Eat Your Vegetables" in *The Action Bible*. Read 1 Corinthians 13:4–8 for additional guidance on living with love.

WHEN YOU WANT TO SERVE

FOR WE ARE GOD'S HANDIWORK, CREATED IN CHRIST JESUS TO DO GOOD WORKS, WHICH GOD PREPARED IN ADVANCE FOR US TO DO.

EPHESIANS 2:10

Nick was discouraged. Several of his friends from church had signed up for the spring break mission trip to serve at the children's camp several hours away. Unfortunately, his family didn't have the money. Not only would his friends be away, but Nick had been excited to serve someplace different. Nick's youth pastor had been talking about God having a plan for him since before He created him, and that he was created to do good works. Even though Nick wasn't able to go on the trip, his leader encouraged him to still serve God here at home. But how?

Paul wrote this verse to the people of Ephesus to explain that we are able to do God's works because God created us, and He has already prepared special things for us to do. In Acts we read about Lydia, a businesswoman in Bible times who sold purple cloth. God worked through Lydia to support Paul in his mission to establish the early church. Lydia had a different role from Paul, but both roles were extremely important to God's bigger plans.

- What should your service look like? You're busy with school and activities. Surely God will understand if you take a pass because you have so much going on, right? Well, not so much. There are countless ways to serve:

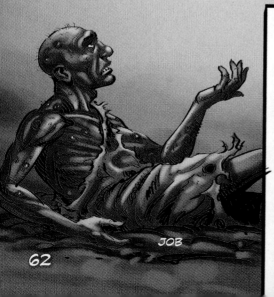

JOB

DISCIPLES IN STORM

the possibilities range from opening a door, to helping a friend or classmate with schoolwork, to going on a mission trip with your church. All acts of service matter to God.

- Be honest with God: FATHER, I AM STUCK. I WANT TO SERVE YOU, BUT I DON'T KNOW WHERE TO START. PLEASE HELP ME TO BE QUIET AND HEAR YOUR VOICE GUIDING ME TOWARD ACTS OF SERVICE IN YOUR NAME. AMEN.

- God works through His followers and He can work through you too. You might already have ideas on how to serve your school, church, family, or neighborhood. Choose one idea and create a plan of action. If you don't have any ideas, take time to be still. Pray to God and ask Him how He wants to do good works through you.

TAKE IT FURTHER

You can read more about Lydia in "The Next Journey" in *The Action Bible* and Acts 16:11–16 to see how Lydia believed in God, was transformed, and then served Paul and his group as they traveled, starting the early church. Read Psalm 46:10 for encouragement on being still and listening to God.

DAVID & GOLIATH

WHEN YOU FEEL ANGRY

BE KIND AND COMPASSIONATE TO ONE ANOTHER, FORGIVING EACH OTHER, JUST AS IN CHRIST GOD FORGAVE YOU.

EPHESIANS 4:32

Seriously? Did that *really* just happen? Katie made a special effort to include Jess at the lunch table, moving over to make room, but when she got up to get a napkin, Jess shoved her lunch aside and let Chelsea have her seat when she showed up late. Katie felt tears of anger welling up. Why were they being so cruel? She was thinking unkind words in response when Jess called out, "Come squeeze in, Katie! Chelsea has some exciting news for us!" Katie let out a sigh of relief and prayed a quick thank you for her friends and that she hadn't given in to her initial angry reaction.

Jesus came to earth to bring salvation through His death and resurrection. After His resurrection, His remaining disciples traveled and brought the good news of Jesus and His teachings to all the regions they could reach. Jesus' journey had highs and lows just like yours. Because He was human Jesus felt all the emotions you feel: He felt betrayed; He felt sad; He felt angry.

Everyone has high points and low points on any given day. As you journey through each day, pay attention to the good and the bad. Stay in communication

ANGEL & MARY

MIRIAM

with God, through prayer, and share with Him how things are going. He will be faithful to help you get through the hard times.

- Anger is a very real emotion and it can be a hard one to know what to do with. How do you react when you are angry? Are you quick to use words to lash out at people? Do you hold your emotions in and let them simmer until you blow up? Even though emotions can come on you quickly, you can choose to handle them thoughtfully.

- Here's a way to pray: FATHER GOD, WHEN I GET ANGRY, I CAN FEEL OUT OF CONTROL. I WANT TO BE ABLE TO RELEASE MY ANGER AND LEARN HOW TO FORGIVE. PLEASE SHOW ME THE BEST WAYS TO SHOW KINDNESS AND COMPASSION. FORGIVE ME FOR THE TIMES WHEN MY ANGER WAS OUT OF CONTROL. AMEN.

- Create a playlist of worship songs. At times when you feel hurt, wronged, or angry, play your songs to remind you of who God is and His faithful love for you.

TAKE IT FURTHER

You can read about one of the times that Jesus was betrayed in "Passover Problems" in *The Action Bible*. Read James 4:1–11 and see more benefits of turning to God in times of trouble.

ESTHER & KING XERXES

HOW CAN YOU TRUST GOD?

DO NOT BE ANXIOUS ABOUT ANYTHING, BUT IN EVERY SITUATION … PRESENT YOUR REQUESTS TO GOD. AND THE PEACE OF GOD, WHICH TRANSCENDS ALL UNDERSTANDING, WILL GUARD YOUR HEARTS AND YOUR MINDS IN CHRIST JESUS.

PHILIPPIANS 4:6-7

As soon as Mark opened his eyes each morning his worries began. Have you ever felt that way? He had many things to be thankful for as well, but sixth grade was wearing him down. He got nervous in social situations, he wondered if he would ever get taller, he had so many assignments due, there was his upcoming band concert … things were piling up on him.

Anxiety is an uneasiness of mind caused by fear or stress. A certain amount of anxiety can be normal. If you're hiking and come across a snake, you will likely feel anxious. That's a good thing, because it's your body telling you that you might be in danger.

In the Bible, Paul wrote to some people who were very fearful. He reminded them that when they felt anxious, they needed to pray and share their concerns with God. Then God's peace would fill their hearts and guard their minds in the name of Jesus. Paul was speaking from experience; when he wrote these verses, he was under house arrest! This is powerful advice for us today.

DISCIPLES

JONATHAN

Sharing your fears with God and trusting Him can be part of your daily prayers. Be sure to tell God what's on your heart—both the good and the bad.

- It is normal to deal with worries, but if you feel like you are constantly overwhelmed, talk to a trusted adult and be completely honest. Ask for some help to control the anxiety you are feeling. In addition to sharing our fears with God, it's been proven that slow, deep breaths will actually calm anxiety levels.

- Try the following prayer. As you inhale slowly, **LOVING GOD** ... then as you exhale slowly, **BRING ME PEACE.** Repeat several times until you feel your heart rate slowing.

- Ask a trusted family member the following questions for their perspective: When you are afraid, what do you do? If your fears lead to deeper anxiety, how do you handle them? What resources do you have? How do you trust God with your fears when you pray?

TAKE IT FURTHER
You can read encouraging words Jesus shares with His followers in "The Last Command" in *The Action Bible* or read Matthew 28:19–20.

MARY, JOSEPH, & JESUS TO EGYPT

WHEN YOU FEEL IGNORED

DON'T LET ANYONE LOOK DOWN ON YOU BECAUSE YOU ARE YOUNG, BUT SET AN EXAMPLE FOR THE BELIEVERS IN SPEECH, IN CONDUCT, IN LOVE, IN FAITH AND IN PURITY.

1 TIMOTHY 4:12

"You're too young." "Let me talk to your parents first." "Maybe when you get a little older." Sound familiar? It can feel discouraging when you're told you aren't old enough to do something. But you have great ideas too! You want to make things better and help people, but who is listening to you?

In the Bible, Paul was the man who transformed his entire life and traveled all over establishing the early church. He met a young man named Timothy and recognized his potential as a great leader. He assured him that his age wasn't relevant in the work he would come to do. All work on behalf of Christ is important!

As a young follower of Christ, you can follow Timothy's leadership. How can you do that? Your life can be an example to others with the good choices you make, the words you speak, the kind of friend you are, and more. Have courage to trust God and follow His plan for your life.

ZACCHAEUS & JESUS

KING DAVID & ABIGAIL

- As a young person, you may not be in control of many things, but you can make choices in how you live your life: you can choose to show God's love, share your faith, and live a pure life with your body. It won't always be easy, so enlist family and friends to help you. Their support and your support of them will be great encouragement.

- Share the obstacles you face: DEAR GOD, I DON'T ALWAYS FEEL HEARD. STRENGTHEN ME TO LIVE AS AN EXAMPLE OF SOMEONE WHO SEEKS OUT YOUR LIGHT TO SHINE THROUGH ME. GIVE ME COURAGE TO BE MY BEST FOR YOU. AMEN.

- Friends can help you stay strong in your choices. Talk about good choices you want to make and why those commitments are important. How can you keep one another accountable to staying true to your promises? Then you'll be ready to lead!

TAKE IT FURTHER

You can read about Paul meeting Timothy in "The Next Journey" in *The Action Bible*. For more insight into courage, read Deuteronomy 31:6; Joshua 1:9; and 1 Chronicles 28:20.

JOHN THE BAPTIST & JESUS

69

WHEN SOMETHING IS MISSING

ALL SCRIPTURE IS GOD-BREATHED AND IS USEFUL FOR TEACHING, REBUKING, CORRECTING AND TRAINING IN RIGHTEOUSNESS, SO THAT THE SERVANT OF GOD MAY BE THOROUGHLY EQUIPPED FOR EVERY GOOD WORK.

2 TIMOTHY 3:16–17

Erin had been texting with her cousin, Olivia. Erin couldn't shake the feeling that something was missing in her life. Although she tried to be nice to everyone, excelled at running, got incredible grades, and loved playing the flute in youth orchestra, could there be more? Olivia always seemed to be content. What was the difference? As they continued to chat, they realized that although Erin loved to read, she chose only online articles, gossip blogs, and a few books, but never the Bible.

Olivia suggested they read the Bible together, starting with one chapter of one book, each day. Erin agreed to give it a try and within a couple of weeks, she noticed a difference in how she felt. Not only was she reading Scripture, she was praying more as well. Her relationship with God began to grow, resulting in stronger trust in Him.

You're old enough to choose what you read. The Bible is a solid choice for teaching and equipping a life filled with joy, love, and service. When you spend

JACOB & ISAAC

TIMOTHY

time in God's Word, you will know God's plan for your life. Find someone to read it with you!

- You build a relationship by spending time with someone. We were created to be in a relationship with our Creator. Grow to know God through prayer, time in silence listening to Him, worship, and in community with other believers.

- Here's a way you can pray: CREATOR GOD, YOU MADE ME AND I KNOW THAT YOU LOVE ME. I AM GRATEFUL TO KNOW YOU AND I WANT TO SPEND MORE TIME WITH YOU. PLEASE GIVE ME A GENTLE REMINDER TO STAY CLOSE TO YOU. AMEN.

- A grow challenge for your relationship with God: read your Bible daily. Start with *The Action Bible*. After reading an interesting story, look it up in a full Bible to learn even more. Use the index at the back of *The Action Bible* or the table of contents at the beginning as helpful tools.

TAKE IT FURTHER

You can see Paul's letter to Timothy in "Fight the Good Fight" in *The Action Bible*. Read Psalm 25:4–5 and Psalm 86:11 to dive deeper into what it means to learn from Scripture.

SAMARITAN WOMAN
& JESUS

WHEN YOU ARE IN PAIN

CONSIDER IT PURE JOY, MY BROTHERS AND SISTERS, WHENEVER YOU FACE TRIALS OF MANY KINDS, BECAUSE YOU KNOW THAT THE TESTING OF YOUR FAITH PRODUCES PERSEVERANCE. LET PERSEVERANCE FINISH ITS WORK SO THAT YOU MAY BE MATURE AND COMPLETE, NOT LACKING ANYTHING.

JAMES 1:2-4

Sarah was twelve years old and suffered from horrible migraine headaches. Sometimes the pain was so intense that Sarah asked her mom to take her to the emergency room. She had to miss activities with her friends, which made her feel down. Sarah's grandmother knew the Bible well and shared these verses from James with her.

But her headaches hurt so much! It made her angry at God for letting her suffer. Her grandmother said her faith was being tested, and she showed incredible courage by sharing her feelings honestly. God wants to hear the good and the bad as it happens.

During a busy time of Jesus' teaching, He performed many miracles. One day, a very sick woman knew Jesus would be walking by and reached out to touch His robe, hoping to find healing just by being near Him. Jesus stopped and asked who had touched Him and why. The woman was scared but, with great courage,

ESAU

LEAH & RACHEL

stepped forward. Jesus healed her and sent her to share her story with others. The woman had faith in Jesus and courage to approach Him.

- It's okay to get frustrated with God. Tests of your faith will strengthen your relationship with God and help you persevere when other hard things happen. It takes courage to be honest with God, just like any relationship with a good friend or parent.

- God wants you to bring things to Him like this: FATHER GOD, WHEN THINGS GET HARD, WHEN I EXPERIENCE PAIN, HELP ME SEE THE GOOD SO I CAN GROW IN MY FAITH IN YOU. GIVE ME THE COURAGE TO SEEK YOU SO I CAN HANDLE ALL THAT LIFE BRINGS. AMEN.

- Think of ways to serve others who might be hurting. Do you like to draw? Can you bake and decorate cupcakes to deliver to local agencies that help families with sick children? Be sure to call first and find out what is accepted and needed. Then gather with friends or family and serve others.

TAKE IT FURTHER

You can read about Jesus healing the sick woman in "Two Miracles" in *The Action Bible*. Read Luke 8:42–48 for the full story of how Jesus healed the sick woman.

JESUS & BOY WITH LUNCH

WHEN SOMEONE ASKS YOU

ALWAYS BE PREPARED TO GIVE AN ANSWER TO EVERYONE WHO
ASKS YOU TO GIVE THE REASON FOR THE HOPE THAT YOU HAVE.
BUT DO THIS WITH GENTLENESS AND RESPECT, KEEPING A CLEAR
CONSCIENCE, SO THAT THOSE WHO SPEAK MALICIOUSLY AGAINST YOUR
GOOD BEHAVIOR IN CHRIST MAY BE ASHAMED OF THEIR SLANDER.

1 PETER 3:15-16

Kyle was excited to be getting new neighbors with kids his age. Their moving truck was being unloaded all morning and he found it fascinating to see their stuff. A car pulled up in front of the house and a boy got out. The boy saw Kyle watching from his bike and came over to introduce himself. "Do you go to church?" the boy asked. Wow! Sure, he and his family went every week, but Kyle had never been asked this question before.

This verse from 1 Peter encourages you to be ready with an answer for anyone who asks why you believe in God. Some call this an "elevator speech," meaning it can be shared quickly, in the length of an elevator ride. Think about why you believe in God and the difference it makes in your life. Why does having this answer ready matter? The way you speak and act leaves a lasting impression with people. When people know you are a Christ follower, you are reflecting God

JESUS, MARY,
& MARTHA

JOSHUA &
PROMISED LAND

74

and showing others what He is like. Choose your words carefully, with kindness, gentleness, and respect.

- To prepare to answer others about your faith, think about your relationship with God. When did you first come to know God? Who taught you about Jesus? How have you experienced God in your daily life? What lessons has God taught you?

- Take time to talk to God: CREATOR GOD, I KNOW THAT YOU LOVE ME. I AM SO GRATEFUL! I WANT TO SHARE YOUR LOVE WITH THE PEOPLE I MEET. GUIDE ME WHEN I SPEAK SO I CAN SHARE MY STORY WITH OTHERS. AMEN.

- Write out your faith journey, answering the above questions. Tell it to someone you trust and then another person. The more you practice, the easier it will be when someone asks you to share the reasons for your faith.

TAKE IT FURTHER
Read about Paul testifying about his faith in "Bound for Rome" in *The Action Bible* or in Acts 23.

MARY & JESUS

JESUS & LAZARUS

WHEN WE SHOW COMPASSION

THE LORD ... SAID IN HIS HEART: "NEVER AGAIN WILL I CURSE THE GROUND BECAUSE OF HUMANS.... AND NEVER AGAIN WILL I DESTROY ALL LIVING CREATURES, AS I HAVE DONE."

GENESIS 8:21

You've seen a rainbow, right? It's pretty cool because rainbows contain all the colors of the light spectrum. But what's also amazing is that they are a symbol of God's promise, one He made thousands of years ago and has kept ever since. God said He would never again destroy all life.

You've probably heard the story: humanity was pretty rotten, so God decided to flood the entire world and start over. But one guy and his family loved God and obeyed Him, so God saved that guy (his name was Noah)—along with two of every animal. They survived the flood in a huge boat (called an ark) Noah built as instructed by God and eventually brought life back to the flooded earth.

God knows people will still turn away from Him, because we are not perfect. We are going to mess up. But He still promises not to destroy everything, even if we deserve it. That's called grace and mercy, and it's a great reminder to you that your response to people who hurt you or are bullies should be like God's. It's amazing what can happen when you show love or compassion to others. It

JESUS & DISCIPLES

JESUS ON DONKEY

can change how you feel about them—and it can even change how they feel about themselves.

- It's really hard to forgive people who hurt us. But nursing a grudge won't make things better. In fact, hanging on to the hurts of the past usually causes more pain! When you see a rainbow in the sky, let it remind you to forgive others, even when they don't deserve it. Jesus set an example for us: forgiveness and mercy, and a whole lot of grace.

- You could tell God this: DEAR GOD, IT'S NOT EASY TO SHOW GRACE OR FORGIVENESS TO PEOPLE WHO HURT ME. PLEASE HELP ME THIS WEEK TO FORGIVE OTHERS. I DON'T WANT TO HOLD GRUDGES BUT TO FOLLOW YOUR EXAMPLE OF GIVING GRACE TO PEOPLE WHO MAY NOT DESERVE IT. THANK YOU, JESUS! AMEN.

- All the colors of the light spectrum are in a rainbow, meaning it takes every color to make one. It also takes people of all kinds to make up the world we live in. When you see a rainbow, remember that God put us in a world filled with people who need to see His love and grace too.

TAKE IT FURTHER

You can read about God's promise after the flood in "A Rainbow Promise" in *The Action Bible*. For more promises, read about a man named Abraham beginning in Genesis 11.

JEZEBEL & ELIJAH

PETER & JESUS

WHEN YOU NEED WISDOM

"SO GIVE YOUR SERVANT A DISCERNING HEART TO GOVERN YOUR PEOPLE AND TO DISTINGUISH BETWEEN RIGHT AND WRONG. FOR WHO IS ABLE TO GOVERN THIS GREAT PEOPLE OF YOURS?"

1 KINGS 3:9

Have you ever thought about what would you ask for if someone came along and offered you anything you wanted? It's a fun thing to think about. Would you want to be a professional athlete with fame and lots of money? Maybe you would ask for a nice house or a new gaming system. Maybe you would request that a family member get well from a sickness. Or for that puppy you've always wanted to cuddle up with at night.

Long ago in the Bible, when King David died, his son Solomon became the new king. One time, Solomon spent all night praying to God. In a dream, God told Solomon to ask for whatever he wanted. What do you think Solomon asked for? Solomon did not ask for wealth or power or long life. Instead, he asked for wisdom to rule the people and to know what was right and wrong. God was pleased with Solomon's request for wisdom and told him that He would also give him a long life, victory over his enemies, and riches!

SAUL & SAMUEL

ANGEL & JACOB

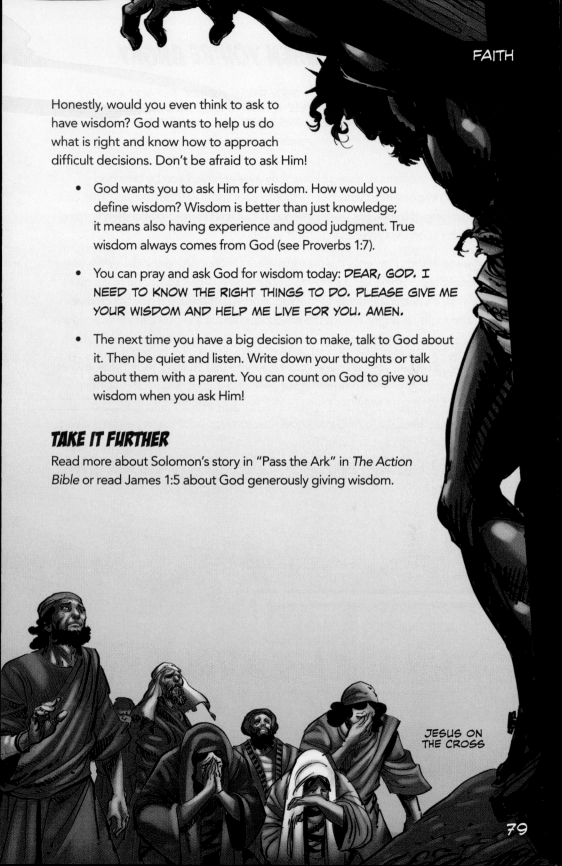

Honestly, would you even think to ask to have wisdom? God wants to help us do what is right and know how to approach difficult decisions. Don't be afraid to ask Him!

- God wants you to ask Him for wisdom. How would you define wisdom? Wisdom is better than just knowledge; it means also having experience and good judgment. True wisdom always comes from God (see Proverbs 1:7).

- You can pray and ask God for wisdom today: DEAR, GOD. I NEED TO KNOW THE RIGHT THINGS TO DO. PLEASE GIVE ME YOUR WISDOM AND HELP ME LIVE FOR YOU. AMEN.

- The next time you have a big decision to make, talk to God about it. Then be quiet and listen. Write down your thoughts or talk about them with a parent. You can count on God to give you wisdom when you ask Him!

TAKE IT FURTHER

Read more about Solomon's story in "Pass the Ark" in *The Action Bible* or read James 1:5 about God generously giving wisdom.

JESUS ON
THE CROSS

FOR TIMES WHEN YOU'RE ANGRY

REFRAIN FROM ANGER AND TURN FROM WRATH; DO NOT FRET—IT LEADS ONLY TO EVIL. FOR THOSE WHO ARE EVIL WILL BE DESTROYED, BUT THOSE WHO HOPE IN THE LORD WILL INHERIT THE LAND.

PSALM 37:8-9

Do you have brothers or sisters? Have they ever annoyed you by breaking something important to you or coming into your room without asking? That can be frustrating. If things get pretty intense, it can lead to yelling and then fighting and pretty soon everyone is angry and upset.

God understands how easy it is for us to react emotionally to things. When you have a big test coming up, it's easy to fret or worry. When someone hurts your feelings, it's understandable to feel sad. And yes, there are many things that can make us angry. It's not the emotions that are the problem. Emotions are natural responses to our circumstances. Then what causes the trouble?

It's when you let your emotions control you. In this psalm, we see what happens when emotions take over, and it's not good. God wants you to put your hope and trust in Him not yourself. If things are troubling you, ask God to help you know how to respond. If something is making you angry, ask Him to calm your spirit.

When you put your hope and trust in Him and don't focus on your feelings alone, what happens? You move on to the good life God promises!

BOY JESUS
IN TEMPLE

- What things cause you to feel strong emotions, especially negative ones? Is it a video game you play? Are there people who bug you? Is it having to do things you don't want to? How can you respond differently when facing these challenges? (Hint: ask God to help you control your feelings. He is happy to help you in those times!)

- Talk to God anytime: HEAVENLY FATHER, PLEASE HELP ME! I'M FEELING SO ANGRY RIGHT NOW. I WANT TO TRUST YOU TO HELP ME RESPOND THE RIGHT WAY WHEN THINGS HAPPEN. CALM ME DOWN AND HELP ME REMEMBER THAT YOU ARE IN CONTROL. AMEN.

- The next time you face something tough, refocus your thoughts on God through prayer right away. Ask Him to help you respond in a new way. You might be surprised by the difference it makes!

TAKE IT FURTHER

The Bible has many examples of people who let their emotions control them, and it didn't work out too well. Check out "The Wicked Queen and the Defiant Prophet" in *The Action Bible* or read 1 Kings 16:29—17:6 in the Bible.

JOSEPH & BROTHERS

ADAM & EVE

WHEN LYING SEEMS LIKE A GOOD IDEA

A FALSE WITNESS WILL NOT GO UNPUNISHED, AND WHOEVER POURS OUT LIES WILL NOT GO FREE.

PROVERBS 19:5

Have you ever lied? Maybe you *did* see the kid get bullied but when the teacher asked you lied and said you didn't. Your dad asked you if you did your homework and you said yes so you could play your game. You ripped your brother's favorite shirt and when he found out you acted like you knew nothing about it. Sometimes it's tempting to lie to avoid trouble in the moment.

Proverbs tells us that lying is a trap. What does that mean exactly? In the moment, lying may feel like a way to stay free and out of trouble, but it actually leads to being stuck in a cycle of fear and hiding.

The book of Proverbs is full of wisdom about how to live in a way that honors God and leads to a good life. When you follow God's advice in His Word, you will grow in knowledge. Part of that understanding is having integrity (meaning honesty and consistency) and living in a way that pleases God every day.

NAAMAN &
SERVANT GIRL

- Being honest requires strength. Do you consistently tell the truth even when it means getting in trouble? Admitting to the teacher you cheated on the test or fessing up to your brother when you ruined his stuff can be really hard to do. But God is always with you, helping you do what is right.

- Ask God to help you be truthful: DEAR, GOD. YOU ARE A GOD OF TRUTH. I WANT TO BE MORE LIKE YOU BY TELLING THE TRUTH IN EVERY SITUATION. HELP ME AVOID THE LYING TRAP. THANK YOU FOR OFFERING ME STRENGTH AND FORGIVENESS THROUGH JESUS. AMEN.

- Look for ways to tell the truth this week. When someone asks what happened, give an accurate report. When you're tempted to lie, choose honesty instead. You will honor God and others will know they can trust you.

TAKE IT FURTHER

Read the story of Ananias and Sapphira in "A Grave Lie" in *The Action Bible* or read Colossians 3:9–10, which talks about why followers of Jesus shouldn't want to lie.

JESUS & BLIND MAN

NOAH & ANIMALS

WHEN YOU CAN GIVE

WHOEVER IS KIND TO THE POOR LENDS TO THE LORD, AND HE WILL REWARD THEM FOR WHAT THEY HAVE DONE.

PROVERBS 19:17

Kelly had thought about sponsoring a child through the ministry but didn't have quite enough money. Maybe if the whole class donated they would be able to adopt a friend in another country. There is so much need in the world, surely something could be done.

Once there was a woman named Ruth. She and her mother-in-law, Naomi, were alone after their husbands died, so they traveled back to Naomi's homeland of Israel. Ruth went with other poor women to the fields and picked up extra grain the workers dropped.

It was in Boaz's field that Ruth tirelessly collected grain from morning until night. Boaz noticed Ruth and asked his workers about her. Boaz was kind to Ruth and told her to continue to glean in his field. Then he told his workers to pull out extra grain from what they collected for her to pick up. Throughout the harvest, Boaz made sure that Ruth had all the food she needed. Later Boaz took Ruth to be his wife and they had a son. God blessed Boaz for his generosity to Ruth and Naomi.

JOSHUA & WALL OF JERICHO

PRODIGAL SON & FATHER

Does it really make a difference to help one person when there are millions of hurting people in the world? It can feel overwhelming.

- God wants us to care for those who are hurting. In fact, Scripture says giving to someone who is in need is like lending to God! Part of following Jesus is caring about the poor and helping them. When you remember that everything you have actually belongs to God, it's easy to give it away to someone who needs it. He is the One who provides for us when we are generous toward those in need.

- Pray and ask God to show you how to help: DEAR, GOD. HELP ME TO BE GENEROUS TO THOSE WHO HAVE LITTLE. SHOW ME WAYS I CAN HELP THEM. AMEN.

- Read Proverbs 19:17 to your parents and talk about some ways you could be generous to others. Maybe you could collect items for a shelter or earn money to give to a child living in a poor country.

TAKE IT FURTHER

Read about a man who struggled with sharing his wealth in "The Rich Young Ruler" in *The Action Bible* or in Matthew 19:16–30.

ABRAHAM, SARAH, & ISAAC

85

WHEN YOU CAN'T SEE A SOLUTION

WHEN JESUS LOOKED UP AND SAW A GREAT CROWD COMING TOWARD HIM, HE SAID TO PHILIP, "WHERE SHALL WE BUY BREAD FOR THESE PEOPLE TO EAT?" HE ASKED THIS ONLY TO TEST HIM, FOR HE ALREADY HAD IN MIND WHAT HE WAS GOING TO DO.

JOHN 6:5-6

Have you ever had a problem that you just couldn't figure out how to solve? And not just a math problem either. A big dilemma with no solution and everyone counting on you? It's a lot of pressure isn't it? One day the disciples had to come up with food for more than five thousand people. Jesus had been teaching all day, and now it was lunchtime. All the people who had been hanging on His every word were ready to eat and there wasn't a food truck in sight.

Jesus looked at His disciple, Philip, and asked him where he was going to get food for everyone. Philip was immediately stuck on how much money it would take to feed all those people. Thankfully, Andrew found a kid who had brought his sack lunch, and Jesus took it from there!

When faced with a problem, the obvious answer isn't always the solution. In order to solve a problem, sometimes it helps to adjust your point of view. Don't

SAMSON & DELILAH

JESUS & HEALED WOMAN

give up. When it's your turn to solve a problem, trust God to help you! Jesus did it through the boy and his lunch. He can do it for you too.

- You will encounter problems in your life. At times they will be your problems and at times they will be situations caused by others. Think through different solutions and ask people you trust. God can use your idea to help make a difference. God uses what we bring Him.

- Finish this prayer silently: DEAR JESUS, SHOW ME WAYS TO SOLVE PROBLEMS AND BUILD MY TRUST IN YOU. WHEN I'M FACING ... HELP ME REMEMBER THAT YOU CAN USE ME AND MY IDEAS TO POINT OTHERS TO KNOW YOU. AMEN.

- The next time you or your friends face a challenging situation, be tough and don't give up. Talk to God and then look for an answer, even if it's unusual. Trust that God will use what you bring to make things right—then thank Him!

TAKE IT FURTHER

Read the whole story of feeding the five thousand in "A Hungry Crowd" in *The Action Bible* and in John 6:5–13.

MOSES & RED SEA

WHEN YOU GET TIRED OF THE RULES

LET EVERYONE BE SUBJECT TO THE GOVERNING AUTHORITIES, FOR THERE IS NO AUTHORITY EXCEPT THAT WHICH GOD HAS ESTABLISHED. THE AUTHORITIES THAT EXIST HAVE BEEN ESTABLISHED BY GOD.

ROMANS 13:1

Let's admit it: it's not always fun being a kid. There are so many rules. At home, at school, at church. You have adults and leaders everywhere telling you what you can and can't do. It'd be nice if you could just do your own thing and enjoy life, right?

The thing is, there will be rules all your life. If we lived in a world without rules or laws, it'd be chaos. Rules and laws are there to make sure we do the right thing, and they protect us and give us clear direction when we aren't sure what the wise choice may be. Here's what's important to know: this verse from Romans says that God made the world this way!

While we may not always like or agree with who's in charge, God expects us to honor and respect our leaders. You may not like your parents' decisions about video games or what you can look at online, but you still need to respect them and their rules. You may not enjoy the rules your teacher has for the classroom, but God is the one who allowed your teacher to be *your* teacher. He has a reason for it, so you need to trust Him and honor your teacher.

When you feel like ignoring a rule because it's unfair, remember that God knows what is best for you. Talk to Him about what is bothering you and trust Him. (If

PAUL & BLINDING LIGHT

DEBORAH & BARAK

you are being abused by anyone in authority over you, talk to a trusted adult immediately.)

- You probably hear people talking about political leaders at home. Even if you don't like the people who are in government, God wants you to show them proper respect and appreciation—with your words and your attitude.

- You could pray like this: DEAR JESUS, HELP ME RESPECT MY TEACHERS AND PARENTS. REMIND ME TO SHOW THEM HONOR BECAUSE YOU PUT THEM IN MY LIFE FOR A REASON. THANK YOU FOR THEM AND GIVE THEM WISDOM! AMEN!

- Encourage your friends and siblings to show honor and respect to the people in charge around you. Write your teacher a thank-you note, make your mom a card, or just follow directions with a good attitude. Showing honor to leaders will spread to those around you!

TAKE IT FURTHER

Read the story of the disciples in the temple after Jesus' resurrection in "Stand Up for Jesus" in *The Action Bible*. While Peter (along with James and John) took a big stand for Jesus, they still respected the leaders in charge.

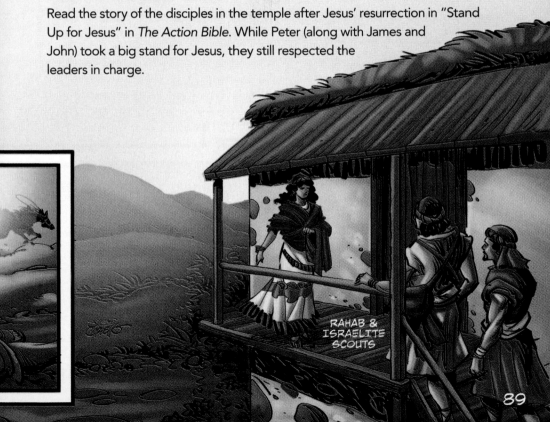

RAHAB & ISRAELITE SCOUTS

SOMETIMES YOU WILL BE TEMPTED

*BECAUSE HE HIMSELF SUFFERED WHEN HE WAS TEMPTED,
HE IS ABLE TO HELP THOSE WHO ARE BEING TEMPTED.*

HEBREWS 2:18

It doesn't matter who you are, where you live, or how old you are, you will find yourself in moments when you will have to choose to do what is right—or not. Temptation is something we all face, even though it looks different for everyone. One person may be tempted to eat a cookie when a parent said to eat a carrot. One person may want to play a video game that's not parent-approved. Maybe another will think about lying to cover up a mistake.

Temptations happen. All the time. It doesn't matter how much you love God, whether you pray every day, or if you read your Bible. So how do you fight it? Good news! You are not alone. In this verse from Hebrews, we see that Jesus is in your corner when those temptation moments come. You see, *He gets it*. He was tempted by the devil with things that looked pretty good at the time—even though it would have gone against what God wanted for Jesus.

Jesus resisted temptation. He used Scripture to remind Himself (and the enemy) what was true and right. So Jesus knows what it feels like to be given the choice, and if you lean into Him in those moments, you can also resist temptation. You

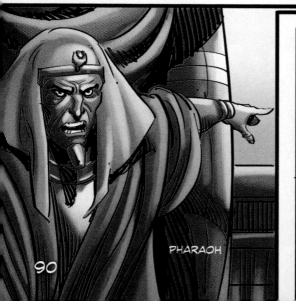

PHARAOH

PAUL'S SHIPWRECK

aren't alone in those times when you feel weak. You have an expert on your side, and He will be there *every single time*. You just need to ask for His help!

- It's important to realize that Jesus didn't beat the temptations just because He is God. He used the same tools you have to resist those tempting moments: Scripture and prayer. You don't have to be God to push back, you just have to use the tools God has given you. Rely on Jesus to give you the assistance you need. He'll be there to help.

- When you're feeling alone: DEAR JESUS, THANK YOU FOR THE GREAT EXAMPLE YOU GIVE FOR FIGHTING TEMPTATION. BE WITH ME IN THOSE MOMENTS, SUCH AS WHEN.... THANK YOU FOR HELPING ME DO THE RIGHT THING! AMEN.

- Jesus fought temptation by speaking a verse to fit what He was fighting. The Bible has many great verses to help you when facing temptation moments. Choose a couple to start memorizing this week. Be ready with verses and know ahead of time what your boundaries are for certain decisions. It may help you decide when you are tempted.

TAKE IT FURTHER

Read the story of Jesus' temptation in "Tempted in the Desert" in *The Action Bible* or in Matthew 4:1–11.

BOAZ & RUTH
IN FIELD

WHEN HUMILITY IS HARD

WHO IS WISE AND UNDERSTANDING AMONG YOU? LET
THEM SHOW IT BY THEIR GOOD LIFE, BY DEEDS DONE
IN THE HUMILITY THAT COMES FROM WISDOM.

JAMES 3:13

Tyler was so annoying! He was acting like such a know-it-all! He always had an answer or piece of advice for everything and behaved like … well, he knew everything. Of course, Tyler cared and believed he was sharing helpful info, but nobody knows everything. It was especially bad when it was obvious that he was wrong or just making up stuff. What does God want you to do with someone like this in your life?

The Bible tells us that Christians are known by their fruit, or the good things they do through knowing Christ (Matthew 7:16). People who are actually wise and understanding are easy to spot because they consistently do good and show humility. That means they don't look for recognition and just quietly help people. Even Jesus, who is God, was humble. He served others and did not brag about the fact that He knew everything (even though He really did).

DANIEL & LIONS

MARY, JOSEPH,
& BABY JESUS

- Does this sound familiar at all? Could you be a bit of a know-it-all? Do you do good things without bragging? Or do you like to prove how smart you are? When you selflessly do these things, you honor God and show true wisdom and understanding.

- Ask God for guidance: DEAR GOD, HELP ME DO THE GOOD THINGS YOU WANT WITH THE RIGHT ATTITUDE. GIVE ME WISDOM AND UNDERSTANDING. HELP ME LIVE IN A WAY THAT IS PLEASING TO YOU. AMEN.

- Look for ways to follow Jesus' humble example this week. When others talk, listen carefully rather than waiting for your turn to speak. Help others without expecting to be noticed or praised. Give up something you want and allow someone else to have it. As you serve with a humble attitude, you become the person God wants you to be!

TAKE IT FURTHER

Joseph's humbling trials taught him to rule with wisdom. You can check out the conclusion of Joseph's story in "Family Reunion" in *The Action Bible* or in Genesis 45–47.

JONAH & FISH

WHEN TEMPERS FLARE

ALL OF YOU, BE LIKE-MINDED, BE SYMPATHETIC, LOVE ONE ANOTHER, BE COMPASSIONATE AND HUMBLE. DO NOT REPAY EVIL WITH EVIL OR INSULT WITH INSULT. ON THE CONTRARY, REPAY EVIL WITH BLESSING, BECAUSE TO THIS YOU WERE CALLED SO THAT YOU MAY INHERIT A BLESSING.

1 PETER 3:8-9

Why did Danny call Mike that name? Everyone was having a good time, but then all of a sudden he had to ruin everything! Did he misunderstand that joke? Everything got intense so quickly. There were more names, then that fight! When the dust settled, nobody won and everyone felt bad. How did it even get started?

This is what Peter was talking about in this verse. He knew what it was like to be called names. After Jesus' resurrection, Peter became the leader of the church and was thrown in prison. He was made fun of and eventually even killed for following Jesus. It's easier to shove someone than it is to walk away, but Peter learned to respond in love and kindness when people tried to hurt him.

If you can live showing humility and compassion to people, you can change the world. This may sound crazy, but it's exactly how Peter and the rest of the disciples lived. It was hard and didn't always mean things turned out with a happy ending, but by loving others and repaying good for evil, they changed how people lived forever.

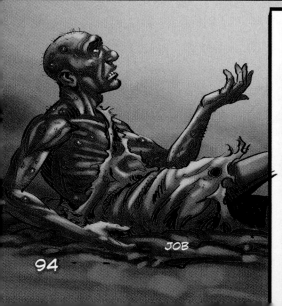

JOB

DISCIPLES IN STORM

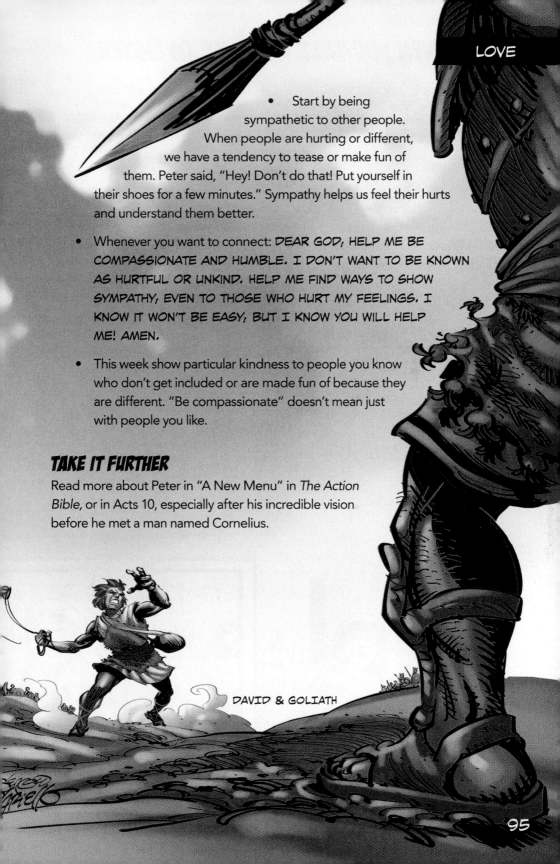

- Start by being sympathetic to other people. When people are hurting or different, we have a tendency to tease or make fun of them. Peter said, "Hey! Don't do that! Put yourself in their shoes for a few minutes." Sympathy helps us feel their hurts and understand them better.

- Whenever you want to connect: DEAR GOD, HELP ME BE COMPASSIONATE AND HUMBLE. I DON'T WANT TO BE KNOWN AS HURTFUL OR UNKIND. HELP ME FIND WAYS TO SHOW SYMPATHY, EVEN TO THOSE WHO HURT MY FEELINGS. I KNOW IT WON'T BE EASY, BUT I KNOW YOU WILL HELP ME! AMEN.

- This week show particular kindness to people you know who don't get included or are made fun of because they are different. "Be compassionate" doesn't mean just with people you like.

TAKE IT FURTHER

Read more about Peter in "A New Menu" in *The Action Bible,* or in Acts 10, especially after his incredible vision before he met a man named Cornelius.

DAVID & GOLIATH

WHEN YOU TAKE THE TIME TO LISTEN

HE TOOK HIM OUTSIDE AND SAID, "LOOK UP AT THE SKY AND COUNT THE STARS—IF INDEED YOU CAN COUNT THEM." THEN HE SAID TO HIM, "SO SHALL YOUR OFFSPRING BE." ABRAM BELIEVED THE LORD, AND HE CREDITED IT TO HIM AS RIGHTEOUSNESS.

GENESIS 15:5-6

Do you ever have a hard time paying attention in class? There can be so many distractions with people talking and making jokes, or the topic might not be as interesting as your own thoughts. The same thing can happen when your mom and dad are talking to you. But when you focus and really listen, there's often important information to hear!

Abram lived long ago and grew to have strong faith in God. God spoke to him many times and His voice to Abram was clear. Because Abram listened, God continued to speak to him. The Lord told Abram to leave his country and his people and go to where God directed him. God guided, Abram obeyed, and God blessed him. When you have strong faith, it's easier to be obedient to God's leading in your life.

ANGEL & MARY

MIRIAM

- How often do you stop and try to listen to God? God's voice was clear to Abram, and it can also be clear to you. Take time each day to stop your activities, quiet your thoughts, and listen to the voice of God. How can you listen? Reading the Bible, praying, or worshipping. Listen as you silence the busyness around you.

- In the quiet, speak to God like this: DEAR GOD, I WANT TO HAVE STRONG FAITH LIKE ABRAM. PLEASE GIVE ME PATIENCE TO BE QUIET AND HEAR WHAT YOU HAVE FOR ME. AMEN.

- When is your best time to listen for God? List each of your daily activities, starting with waking up and ending with going to bed. God can talk to you at anytime, but you can also schedule time to listen to Him. Follow through and spend daily time listening for one week, then another. Soon it will be a new habit and your relationship with God will grow.

TAKE IT FURTHER

You can read God's words to Abram in "Insufficient Sons" in *The Action Bible* or read Genesis 15 to see how his faith impacted the world.

ESTHER &
KING XERXES

WHEN JEALOUSY THREATENS

BUT JOSEPH SAID TO THEM, "DON'T BE AFRAID. AM I IN THE PLACE OF GOD? YOU INTENDED TO HARM ME, BUT GOD INTENDED IT FOR GOOD TO ACCOMPLISH WHAT IS NOW BEING DONE, THE SAVING OF MANY LIVES."

GENESIS 50:19–20

Ryan and Sean were becoming increasingly jealous of their brother, Jordan. The three brothers had wrestled with one another since they could walk. The youngest, Jordan, seemed to have the most natural wrestling ability and won more matches than his older brothers. They hated to admit it, but they wished he would lose occasionally. Ryan and Sean loved their little brother, but it drove them crazy that they could never beat him.

What if you had eleven older brothers who were jealous of you? Joseph had to deal with brothers who hated him so much that they betrayed him and *sold* him. Then he ended up in prison because of someone's lies. But through it all, Joseph kept his faith in God and persevered under hard circumstances. Joseph showed incredible strength through God and became a great leader. Later in life, he even helped his brothers.

DISCIPLES

JONATHAN

- If you have siblings, you can probably relate to the feelings of Ryan, Sean, and Jordan. Jealousy can easily rise up, and people make decisions that are hurtful to people they care about. Can you think of a time when you made a choice and needed forgiveness? It takes great strength to admit when you need forgiveness.

- You could pray like this: GOD, I WANT TO HAVE STRENGTH LIKE JOSEPH BUT SOMETIMES I GET JEALOUS. PLEASE GUIDE ME AND BE CLOSE WHEN I FEEL ANGRY AND JEALOUS TOWARD OTHER PEOPLE. FORGIVE ME AND HELP ME FOCUS ON WHAT YOU HAVE GIVEN ME. AMEN.

- Gather some friends or family members and ask them to share about times when they have been jealous and the strength it takes to keep it under control. Share how God is there for you.

TAKE IT FURTHER

You can read Joseph's story starting with his brothers in "Big Dreams" in *The Action Bible* and how he later helped them in "The End of an Era." Read Exodus 15:2 and Psalm 18:32 for examples of the importance of relying on God's strength.

MARY, JOSEPH, & JESUS TO EGYPT

WHEN YOU'RE FULL OF DOUBT

THE LORD SAID TO HIM, "WHO GAVE HUMAN BEINGS THEIR MOUTHS? WHO MAKES THEM DEAF OR MUTE? WHO GIVES THEM SIGHT OR MAKES THEM BLIND? IS IT NOT I, THE LORD? NOW GO; I WILL HELP YOU SPEAK AND WILL TEACH YOU WHAT TO SAY."

EXODUS 4:11-12

Have you ever signed up for something and then regretted it? Liz's friend talked her into doing the hike and overnight campout, but now her friend couldn't go and Liz was dreading it. How was she going to make it up that trail? She was terrified! And then sleeping in a tent all night? She had rarely slept away from home. What if she did something embarrassing in her sleep or felt so homesick she had to call her parents to come get her in the middle of the night? She wasn't going to survive. But the deposit was paid, and Liz was stuck.

God spoke to Moses because He had a job for him. God didn't mind that Moses wasn't perfect. No one is. God used imperfect people throughout the Bible—and He still does. But Moses doubted he was the right man for the job. He didn't believe he was good enough to be God's spokesman to Pharaoh. By not believing in God's ability to use him, Moses lacked hope.

The verses above are God's words to Moses after God chose him to go to Pharaoh and ask for the release of God's people from slavery. God showed Moses many signs and told Moses He would teach him what to say. God would be with him in his doubt.

ZACCHAEUS & JESUS

KING DAVID & ABIGAIL

- Do you ever experience doubt? How do you handle it? Doubt is one of Satan's favorite tools to use against God's people. Why would that be? Talk to God and tell Him what you are feeling. Then have hope that God will be with you and guide you through the challenges you face. God is always with you, just like He was with Moses. You can listen to God and He will reassure you.

- You could tell God this: GOD, SOMETIMES I FORGET TO COME TO YOU WHEN I HAVE A PROBLEM OR A CHALLENGE. WHEN I DON'T FEEL GOOD ENOUGH, PLEASE ENCOURAGE ME AND HELP ME REMEMBER THAT YOU CREATED ME AND YOU ARE ALWAYS WITH ME. AMEN.

- Write out the words God speaks to Moses in Exodus 4:11–12. Display it somewhere prominent, such as on your bedside table or the bathroom mirror. It can remind you that God created you and is always near.

TAKE IT FURTHER

You can read about Moses meeting God in "A Burning Bush!" in *The Action Bible* or Exodus 2–4.

JOHN THE BAPTIST & JESUS

WHEN IT'S TIME TO CONFESS

SO THEY ASKED HIM, "TELL US, WHO IS RESPONSIBLE FOR MAKING ALL THIS TROUBLE FOR US? ..." HE ANSWERED, "I AM A HEBREW AND I WORSHIP THE LORD, THE GOD OF HEAVEN, WHO MADE THE SEA AND THE DRY LAND."

JONAH 1:8-9

Have you ever been in a situation where things went wrong because of something you did? It's a bad enough place to be, but then you get that feeling in your stomach too. You're all upset and queasy because you just know everyone is going to find out that *you're* to blame. Yeah, that's the worst.

Maybe you've heard of Jonah. He was in that place. Jonah was a prophet of God who was called to an important job, but he decided he didn't agree with God's instructions so he didn't follow them. Instead, he tried to run away, and it only caused a lot of trouble for a bunch of people. An entire boat of sailors were caught in the middle of a storm sent by God, and they figured out Jonah was the reason.

Jonah did the right thing. In spite of being afraid and nervous, he confessed it was his fault; he was to blame. They threw Jonah out of the boat, he was

JACOB & ISAAC

TIMOTHY

swallowed by a big fish (but that's another story), and things calmed down. Being honest may hurt, but it's always the right decision.

- You can't run away from trouble, especially if you're the cause of it. Instead, be honest. Tell the truth and face the consequences. God will give you the strength you need, and you'll feel much better knowing you did the right thing.

- You can always talk to God: DEAR GOD, HELP ME CONFESS WHEN I'M TO BLAME. I KNOW YOU LOVE HONESTY, SO I WANT TO TELL THE TRUTH. HELP ME BE READY TO DEAL WITH WHAT'S NEXT AND TO KNOW THAT YOU'RE WITH ME ALWAYS. AMEN.

- If you need to go back to someone and make up for a situation you caused, don't wait. God knows we all need help in this area, and He gives us what we need to do it. Although it may be messy, you'll feel better once you confess, and others will discover that you are someone who tells the truth.

TAKE IT FURTHER
Read the story of Jonah in "A Fishy Story" in *The Action Bible* and in the book of Jonah in the Bible.

SAMARITAN WOMAN & JESUS

WHEN YOU FEEL TRAPPED

MOSES ANSWERED THE PEOPLE, "DO NOT BE AFRAID. STAND FIRM AND YOU WILL SEE THE DELIVERANCE THE LORD WILL BRING YOU TODAY.... THE LORD WILL FIGHT FOR YOU; YOU NEED ONLY TO BE STILL."

EXODUS 14:13-14

Mark was a quiet boy and was often teased because his classmates thought he looked different. One day a group of kids chased Mark to the edge of the park and were saying awful things and calling him names. Mark felt trapped, but he knew the story of Moses and God's people. Mark took a deep breath, said a quick prayer, and asked God to give him strength to handle the situation. Mark looked at the kids and simply told them that their actions and words were hurting his feelings and it wasn't okay.

Moses knew the feeling of being trapped. He led God's people to flee Egypt and make it all the way to the Red Sea where the Lord told Moses to camp. Pharaoh and his entire army were in chariots chasing them and God's people felt trapped. They cried out to Moses and Moses shared the words from Exodus 14 with them. He told them to be strong and trust that God would take care of them.

ESAU

LEAH & RACHEL

- Has anything in your life seemed so desperate that you felt you were trapped or under attack? Sometimes kids like to gang up on others, teasing them or pushing them around. That's a form of bullying, and it's not okay. When things feel like they are closing in, remember that "the LORD will fight for you; you need only to be still" (Exodus 14:14). If you are experiencing bullying, be sure to talk to a trusted adult and ask for help. God puts people in your life for a reason, and it might be to help you through a tough situation.

- God hears you when you talk to Him: FATHER, YOU WERE WITH MOSES AND ALL YOUR PEOPLE WHEN PHARAOH CHASED THEM. YOU PROVIDED THE WAY OUT FOR THEM WHEN THEY PATIENTLY TRUSTED YOU. I NEED THAT SAME STRENGTH. I AM GLAD YOU ARE ALWAYS WITH ME. AMEN.

- Pay attention in the coming days to the people around you. Look for someone who might need a friend because she is being left out, made fun of, or bullied. Make an effort to include that person so she doesn't feel trapped in her situation.

TAKE IT FURTHER

For another story about someone feeling very trapped and needing strength to wait, read "20,000 Egyptians Under the Sea" in *The Action Bible* or Exodus 14.

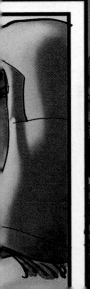

JESUS & BOY WITH LUNCH

105

WHY WON'T YOU STOP IT?

THE LORD IS COMPASSIONATE AND GRACIOUS, SLOW TO ANGER, ABOUNDING IN LOVE. HE WILL NOT ALWAYS ACCUSE, NOR WILL HE HARBOR HIS ANGER FOREVER.... FOR AS HIGH AS THE HEAVENS ARE ABOVE THE EARTH, SO GREAT IS HIS LOVE FOR THOSE WHO FEAR HIM; AS FAR AS THE EAST IS FROM THE WEST, SO FAR HAS HE REMOVED OUR TRANSGRESSIONS FROM US.

PSALM 103:8-9, 11-12

Brothers. They can be your best friends, and they can also get on your last nerve. The Johnson brothers were like that. The older brother was very serious and liked to follow a schedule with everything planned out and orderly. This actually brought him great peace in life, because he always knew what was coming next. The younger brother was quite the opposite. He preferred no structure, jumping from one activity to the next with no planning at all. You can imagine that this attitude often rubbed his older brother the wrong way, resulting in conflict within the family.

Mrs. Johnson worked hard to teach her sons the value of patience and she liked to share Bible verses to encourage them. By explaining their differences to one another, she hoped the boys would appreciate and value the traits in the other that they didn't readily relate to.

Two famous brothers in the Bible were Isaac and Esau. They were opposites in nearly every way, from their interests to how they looked. They had a bitter disagreement that kept them apart for many, many years.

JESUS, MARY, & MARTHA

JOSHUA & PROMISED LAND

Compassion and grace are important in any relationship, but especially with family members.

- At times, having the patience to show your siblings grace and forgiveness can be challenging. Remember: all skills in life take practice. Try to listen more and see the other person's side of things. Make eye contact, hear what your sibling says, and repeat her words (in a nice way!) to be sure you understand. (For example: I hear you saying that you don't like it when I blast my music from my room.) The more you practice, the more your love and patience skills will grow.

- Take time right now to talk to God: DEAR GOD, IT CAN BE HARD TO LISTEN SOMETIMES. I WANT TO SHOW MORE COMPASSION AND GRACE TO MY FAMILY MEMBERS. PLEASE HELP ME LEARN AND GROW. AMEN.

- Create a saying for when you find yourself losing patience. Some ideas might include, "Look, listen, smile—go that extra mile." "Breathe in, two, three—happier we all will be." Create your own and try it!

TAKE IT FURTHER

Read about two famous brothers—Isaac and Esau—and their battle with patience for each other in "Birthright Stew" in *The Action Bible* or read Genesis 25–26.

MARY & JESUS

JESUS & LAZARUS

WHEN LIFE IS STORMY

Life is full of storms. Each day, you are faced with choices to make: some are simple but some feel scary. What to wear, answers on tests, who to throw the ball to in a game, how to treat a friend, words to use when your sibling frustrates you … the list goes on and on and on. It's not easy!

Hard things may pile up. Some days you may wonder if you're sinking in an ocean of problems.

One day after Jesus taught a large crowd, He needed a break. Jesus instructed the disciples to head out in a boat and He told them He would meet up with them. During the night, they saw something incredible—Jesus walking toward them on the water! Peter immediately jumped out of the boat to meet Jesus. As long as his eyes were on Jesus, he walked on the water as well. But when Peter took his eyes off Jesus, he remembered the wind and the waves, and he began to sink. Jesus immediately pulled him up. Fortunately, not every hard thing that happens is as extreme or as scary as sinking in the ocean! Your faith in God will save you when things get bad.

JESUS &
DISCIPLES

JESUS ON
DONKEY

- "Keep your eyes on Jesus." When Peter focused his attention on Jesus, he was safe above the water. Peter had enough faith to walk out to Jesus. How can you keep your eyes on Jesus and lock into that same strength and faith that Peter had? Keep your relationship with God strong. Talk to Him daily—multiple times a day—in prayer. Learn about God and then spend time in worship and praise. Read stories from the Bible for more examples of people's faith.

- You could pray like this: GOD, I KNOW YOU ARE ALWAYS WITH ME. YOU ARE RIGHT HERE IN GOOD TIMES AND HARD TIMES. THANK YOU FOR LOVING ME SO MUCH THAT YOU NEVER LEAVE ME. AMEN.

- Think about this story and talk about it with family members or friends. Ask them their thoughts: What does it mean to have faith? If you were on the boat with the disciples and saw Jesus walking toward you, how would you react?

TAKE IT FURTHER

You can read about Jesus walking on the water in "Walking on Water" in *The Action Bible* or in Matthew 14:22–33; Mark 6:45–52; and John 6:15–21.

JEZEBEL & ELIJAH

PETER & JESUS

WILL GOD CATCH ME WHEN I FALL?

*TRUST IN THE LORD WITH ALL YOUR HEART AND LEAN NOT
ON YOUR OWN UNDERSTANDING; IN ALL YOUR WAYS SUBMIT
TO HIM, AND HE WILL MAKE YOUR PATHS STRAIGHT.*

PROVERBS 3:5-6

A favorite camp activity is the trust fall. One person is chosen to "fall" and trust his friends to catch him. The person stands, slightly elevated, arms crossed over his chest, with his back to two lines of people who face one another, arm length apart, with all arms held straight in front of them. The trusting person falls straight back into the arms of his friends. This isn't as easy as it sounds. Some people are very hesitant to fall back. Why does it work? Because the person falling lets go and trusts the people will catch him.

Shadrach, Meshach, and Abednego were men who worked for King Nebuchadnezzar. One day this king made an evil decree and the three men, followers of God, would not obey. They were called to the king, tied up, and thrown into a blazing hot furnace as punishment. The men trusted that God was with them. When the king and his men looked into the furnace, they saw four men, not three, unbound and walking around. They were unhurt, protected by God.

SAUL &
SAMUEL

ANGEL
& JACOB

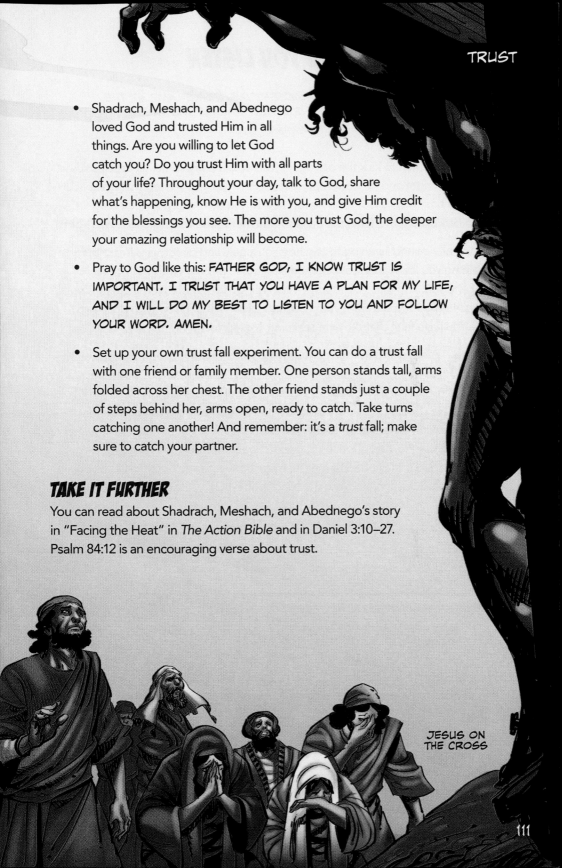

- Shadrach, Meshach, and Abednego loved God and trusted Him in all things. Are you willing to let God catch you? Do you trust Him with all parts of your life? Throughout your day, talk to God, share what's happening, know He is with you, and give Him credit for the blessings you see. The more you trust God, the deeper your amazing relationship will become.

- Pray to God like this: FATHER GOD, I KNOW TRUST IS IMPORTANT. I TRUST THAT YOU HAVE A PLAN FOR MY LIFE, AND I WILL DO MY BEST TO LISTEN TO YOU AND FOLLOW YOUR WORD. AMEN.

- Set up your own trust fall experiment. You can do a trust fall with one friend or family member. One person stands tall, arms folded across her chest. The other friend stands just a couple of steps behind her, arms open, ready to catch. Take turns catching one another! And remember: it's a *trust* fall; make sure to catch your partner.

TAKE IT FURTHER
You can read about Shadrach, Meshach, and Abednego's story in "Facing the Heat" in *The Action Bible* and in Daniel 3:10–27. Psalm 84:12 is an encouraging verse about trust.

JESUS ON
THE CROSS

WHEN YOU LISTEN

*LISTEN TO ADVICE AND ACCEPT DISCIPLINE, AND AT THE
END YOU WILL BE COUNTED AMONG THE WISE.*

PROVERBS 19:20

Nate did *not* want to kick the ball again. This was the fifth time his coach said his form wasn't right and he was embarrassed. However, he trusted that his coach knew the best way to kick it, so he listened to the corrections and tried again. When he kicked it this time, the ball went further than ever! His coach was right!

Getting advice and listening to teachers, coaches, and directors is important in helping you learn and grow. Sometimes, these teachers may correct you or discipline you, and that's not always a bad thing. If you were learning a new sport like Nate, you would want your coach to explain the right way to do things. You have faith that they are teaching you correctly.

There was a Roman centurion or soldier who looked for Jesus on the road as Jesus was traveling and teaching. The soldier's servant was dying. He asked Jesus if He would heal the servant. Jesus asked if He should go to the soldier's home. But the centurion had so much faith in Jesus and His words that he said Jesus could heal the servant from wherever He was; all Jesus had to do was give the command. Jesus acknowledged that He hadn't met many people with such faith in His ability. Jesus healed the servant from the road, right then, without ever seeing him.

BOY JESUS
IN TEMPLE

- What is the difference between *hearing* someone and *listening* to them? When you *hear* something, you register the sounds within your ear and the sound waves are transmitted to your brain. When you *listen*, you take sounds that you hear and use that information to make informed decisions. It might be identifying problems and solutions, learning new things, or taking advice and applying it to make changes. Listen to the advice of teachers, especially Jesus, to grow your knowledge and wisdom.

- Pray this prayer: DEAR GOD, JESUS IS SUCH A GREAT TEACHER. I HAVE FAITH THAT HE WILL TEACH ME IN MY LIFE. PLEASE SHOW ME TIMES WHEN I SHOULD ACCEPT HIS ADVICE AND THE ADVICE OF IMPORTANT PEOPLE IN MY LIFE. AMEN.

- The Roman soldier had incredible faith in Jesus' power to heal his servant. Write down some things that have grown your faith. For example, you can start several sentences with, "My faith in God grew when …"

TAKE IT FURTHER

You can read about the story of the Roman centurion and his incredible faith in "An Officer's Request" in *The Action Bible* and in Matthew 8:5–13.

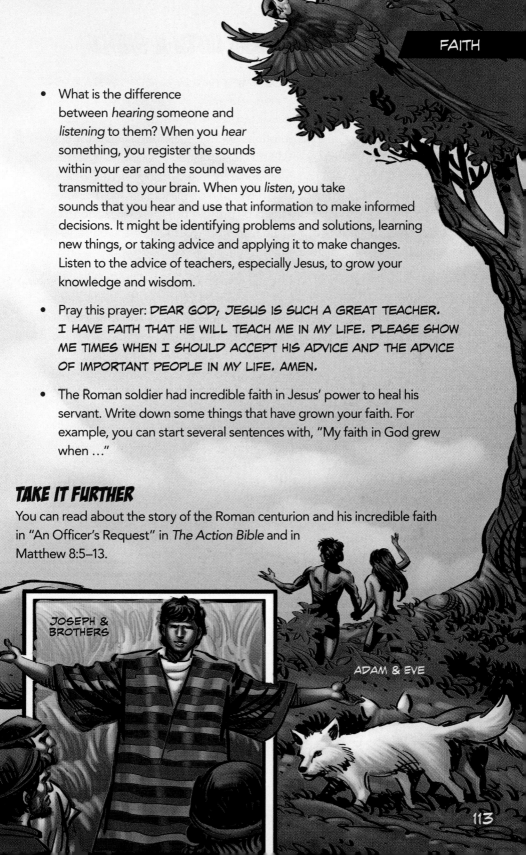

JOSEPH & BROTHERS

ADAM & EVE

WHEN YOU SERVE WITH A SMILE

AS IRON SHARPENS IRON, SO ONE PERSON SHARPENS ANOTHER.
PROVERBS 27:17

Connor loved asking Grandpa questions about life. Grandpa was often surprised at Connor's good questions, and Grandpa's answers were always wise. Grandpa said it was like iron sharpening iron when they talked. Connor asked what that meant. Grandpa explained, "It means one person making the life of another person better. You can sharpen others by the way you live, making good choices, modeling strong integrity, and doing acts of service. And when you serve others, you set an example for all to see God's light shining through you."

Jesus certainly lived a life of service and deeply influenced His disciples. They went on to serve in His name. Near the end of His life on earth, Jesus gathered His disciples for the Passover dinner. The men were weary and dirty from a day of traveling and teaching. It was customary for servants to wash the dirty feet of the guests before a meal was served. However, Jesus chose to wash His disciples' feet that day. They didn't want Jesus to stoop down and do the job of a servant. But Jesus did it anyway. He modeled for His closest friends and followers that even Jesus, the Son of God, came to lower Himself and serve.

NAAMAN &
SERVANT GIRL

- You can serve your family and community as well. Acts of service can range from very simple to more involved. An example of a simple act can be picking up your neighbor's newspapers when they're away on vacation. You can also seek out local organizations that need volunteers or donations such as hospitals, animal shelters, and homeless shelters. Think about your interests and find a place to serve. Grab some friends and a trusted adult to get you started.

- God hears you when you pray: DEAR GOD, I KNOW EVERYONE CAN MAKE A DIFFERENCE. I WANT TO SERVE AND HELP OTHERS IN THE BEST WAY I CAN. PLEASE GUIDE AND DIRECT ME. AMEN.

- Think of the people in your life who serve others and what it is they do that's so special. Thank them for showing you how important it is to serve by sending them notes or thanking them in person.

TAKE IT FURTHER

You can read about Jesus washing the feet of the disciples in "Passover Problems" in *The Action Bible*. Read Matthew 5:16 for encouragement on how God's light can shine through you.

JESUS & BLIND MAN

NOAH & ANIMALS

115

HOW CAN YOU HAVE MORE LIGHT?

THE PEOPLE WALKING IN DARKNESS HAVE SEEN A GREAT LIGHT; ON THOSE LIVING IN THE LAND OF DEEP DARKNESS A LIGHT HAS DAWNED.

ISAIAH 9:2

It was a nice summer day, so John decided to take his bike out for a ride. The hills were fast, the wind blew in his face—life seemed perfect! But before he knew it, John found himself on the ground with a scraped knee and bruised arm. Everything suddenly felt dark and sad. Has something like this ever happened to you?

Every day is filled with light and dark. The sun rises with light and sets, bringing darkness. Sometimes life seems to be filled with light and happiness and God feels like He's right next to you! Other times life might feel heavy or dark. It takes courage to face those dark days.

Isaiah was an Old Testament prophet. A prophet is someone God speaks to and gives a message to share. God spoke to Isaiah and sent him visions to tell God's people. Isaiah listened and shared about the future coming of Jesus. Isaiah talked

JOSHUA & WALL OF JERICHO

PRODIGAL SON & FATHER

about how God's people would be living in darkness until God sent the Savior, Jesus, to bring light to their lives—the light of God.

- Just as God had a plan for Isaiah and all the people of the Bible, God has a plan for you. Think of a dark time in your life. This might include a family member or friend getting sick, someone you know dying, your parents divorcing, getting in a car accident, or even just a time of sadness or loneliness. God has allowed people in the Bible, like Job, to experience extremely hard things. But God was always with Job. Talk to God in prayer; He's there and wants to comfort you.

- Here's a way you can pray: GOD, I AM GLAD YOU LOVE ME AND ARE ALWAYS WITH ME. IT CAN BE HARD TO SEE YOUR LIGHT THROUGH THE DARKNESS. GIVE ME COURAGE TO FOCUS ON YOU. AMEN.

- Invite your parent or another trusted adult to answer the following questions: When have you felt some darkness in your life? Did you feel the presence of God at that time? How can you trust God's light even when things feel dark?

TAKE IT FURTHER

Read about Isaiah in "A Burning Coal" in *The Action Bible*. Read Matthew 5:14–16 for further encouragement on being God's light in the world.

ABRAHAM, SARAH, & ISAAC

WHEN DO YOU PRAY?

THREE TIMES A DAY HE GOT DOWN ON HIS KNEES AND PRAYED, GIVING THANKS TO HIS GOD, JUST AS HE HAD DONE BEFORE.

DANIEL 6:10

Meg couldn't wait to dive into her lunch. Her mom made the best sandwiches, and this cheese and pickle special didn't disappoint. As she happily munched, she noticed her friend from church, Aspen, was closing her eyes and praying over her lunch. Meg felt a quick pang of conviction. Even in the rush of the cafeteria, she knew she should pause to give thanks.

Have you heard the story of Daniel in the lions' den? Daniel was punished by being thrown into a pit full of lions. But God was with him *all* night and the lions left him alone. The king then believed that Daniel's God was the one true God. Do you know why Daniel was punished? For praying! Daniel worked for a king who made a law stating that people could only pray to him. But Daniel loved and trusted God. Talking to God was so important to Daniel that he continued to openly pray to *only* God—three times a day.

Jesus took time daily to talk to His Father, drawing strength and guidance from this personal connection. The disciples saw the value Jesus placed on getting away to be alone with God early in the mornings or even in the evenings after long days of teaching and healing. The disciples asked Jesus how they should pray, and He taught them with what we now call "The Lord's Prayer."

God wants to know you and be close to you. Take a cue from Jesus and make talking to God as easy and natural as reaching out to a friend. Give Him your life and share it all with Him.

SAMSON & DELILAH

JESUS & HEALED WOMAN

- Think for a moment about your prayer life. Are you comfortable praying at anytime? Do you pray only when you need something? Do you share the good things, thanking God? Think of prayer as your time with God. He already knows all about you, but He wants to hear it from you!

- Take a fresh approach to prayer: HELLO, GOD! I'D LIKE TO SPEND MORE TIME WITH YOU. I WANT TO WAKE UP, CHECK IN, AND FILL YOU IN THROUGHOUT MY DAY. FORGIVE ME FOR NOT SPENDING ENOUGH TIME WITH YOU. I WANT MY FAITH TO GROW AS OUR RELATIONSHIP DEEPENS. AMEN.

- Like in Daniel's time, there are places in the world today that don't allow people to openly pray. There are actual laws against it. Along with your family, write down a few laws that support prayer or research countries that limit prayer and pray for the people there. Talk about why prayer is important to you.

TAKE IT FURTHER

You can read about Daniel's commitment to pray to God in "Lion Taming" in *The Action Bible* or in Daniel 6. Jesus taught His disciples a special prayer most Christians know today. Read about it in "The Lord's Prayer" in *The Action Bible* or in Matthew 6:9–13. It's a great prayer to lead your worship to God.

MOSES & RED SEA

HOW DO YOU CHOOSE?

"I SAID, 'YOU ARE MY SERVANT'; I HAVE CHOSEN YOU AND HAVE NOT REJECTED YOU. SO DO NOT FEAR, FOR I AM WITH YOU; DO NOT BE DISMAYED, FOR I AM YOUR GOD."

ISAIAH 41:9-10

How do you feel when you're chosen to read out loud in front of others? How about when a friend asks you to hang out? Or have you ever been picked first to play on a team? Sometimes it feels good to be chosen as the one to do something; other times it can feel scary.

The disciples chose a man named Stephen to continue their work of telling people the good news of salvation through Jesus. Some religious leaders falsely accused Stephen of speaking against God and brought him to the religious court. Stephen answered the accusations confidently and peacefully but they were furious when he calmly looked to the sky and proclaimed that he saw Jesus sitting next to God. The leaders rushed at Stephen, dragged him outside, and stoned him to death.

Stephen put God's glory on display until the very end of his life. If you are a follower of Jesus, God has chosen you. It's not always easy to follow God's ways—to stand up for your faith, to tell the truth, or to apologize when you've done something wrong. It takes courage. Stephen had the courage to say and do the right thing, even when it meant he might die.

You may not face death for your faith, but will you make hard choices? Are you willing to be mocked or give up the chance to be popular?

PAUL & BLINDING LIGHT

DEBORAH & BARAK

- To be chosen by God, to make choices that please Him, to follow Him no matter the cost … these are hard things to understand sometimes. God has created different plans for each of us. Invite God to help you make the best and most courageous decisions.

- Pray this prayer: DEAR GOD, I KNOW THAT YOU HAVE CHOSEN ME. I AM YOURS AND THAT IS A GREAT THING! BLESS ME WITH COURAGE LIKE STEPHEN TO MAKE THE RIGHT CHOICES IN MY DAY. AMEN.

- Together with your friends or family, discuss the following questions: Do you feel chosen by God? Why or why not? How do your choices impact the people around you?

TAKE IT FURTHER

You can read about Stephen's story in "The Stoning" in *The Action Bible* or Acts 6:5–6, 8; 7:55, 59.

RAHAB & ISRAELITE SCOUTS

WHEN YOU WANT TO GET EVEN

"YOU HAVE HEARD THAT IT WAS SAID, 'LOVE YOUR NEIGHBOR AND HATE YOUR ENEMY.' BUT I TELL YOU, LOVE YOUR ENEMIES AND PRAY FOR THOSE WHO PERSECUTE YOU, THAT YOU MAY BE CHILDREN OF YOUR FATHER IN HEAVEN."

MATTHEW 5:43-45

Marco worked hard in school and on his soccer team. He listened well and treated people with kindness. However, Marco was shorter than most kids and was often teased about it. It hurt when his teammates called him names and laughed at him. Sometimes Marco wanted to lash out at the mean kids and try to hurt them the way they hurt him. But his coach advised him to ignore the name-calling and, instead of being mean himself, pray for the kids treating him badly. Although this was hard for Marco, every time he heard an insult he chose to take a deep breath and say a quick prayer for the person.

Over time the kids stopped teasing Marco. They grew to respect him for his strong character and relied on him to hold the team together. As they played, they became friends and some of the boys even apologized for not giving him a chance.

PHARAOH

PAUL'S SHIPWRECK

Jesus shared these verses from Matthew with a crowd that gathered to hear Him teach. Jesus knows it's hard for all of us, but He taught us to love our enemies and be kind to people who treat us badly. Jesus lived this out Himself.

- Loving people who treat you badly can be hard to do, but it keeps you from a cycle of anger and revenge. Practice taking a deep breath and saying a quick prayer for the person who isn't nice. You'll grow closer to God as He hears your prayers. Through praying for your "enemy," you may start to understand why that person acts the way he does. This may lead to you being able to show him God's love.

- When you need to quickly pray for someone who is being unkind, try this prayer: DEAR GOD, HELP (NAME OF PERSON) KNOW YOUR LOVE. AMEN.

- Gather your teammates or friends and discuss the following questions: How do we treat others who are different from us? What are some ways we can encourage kindness? How are we living lives of integrity? What are safe ways to show God's love to those who don't treat us well?

TAKE IT FURTHER

You can read about Jesus' "Sermon on a Mountain" in *The Action Bible*. Or read Matthew 5 and John 13:34 for more commands from Jesus about loving one another.

BOAZ & RUTH
IN FIELD

WHAT WOULD JESUS DO?

"FOLLOW ME," JESUS TOLD HIM, AND LEVI GOT UP AND FOLLOWED HIM.
MARK 2:14

Macy noticed the girl sitting by herself in the cafeteria. Macy had been in that position in third grade when her family moved here. It took awhile before anyone had invited her to sit with them, so she knew how this girl must feel. But what would her friends think if she asked this girl to join them? There wasn't much room, they all knew one another's secrets, and this girl's clothing choices were a little weird. Would her friends be mad at her?

When people are different or new, it can be hard to become their friends. It takes courage to talk to someone nobody likes or who people think is weird. Maybe you think you're that person. Thankfully, Jesus shows us how to love others—no matter who they are or what they do. Did you know that throughout Jesus' teaching, He invited many people who were considered outsiders to become His followers?

Jesus called Levi (a tax collector also called Matthew) to be one of His disciples. Sitting in his booth, doing his job that people hated him for, Matthew was called by Jesus to follow Him. Matthew showed courage by giving up his business. Then Jesus had dinner at Matthew's house with a whole bunch of other tax collectors! People didn't like that Jesus was getting friendly with unpopular people. But every person mattered to Jesus and by speaking to them, healing

DANIEL & LIONS

MARY, JOSEPH, & BABY JESUS

them, and eating and drinking with them, He showed God's love and many people chose to follow Him.

- Are there people in your church or community who seem different or like they don't belong? How can you include them? It definitely takes courage to approach someone who seems unlike you. There is an old term: WWJD?, meaning "What Would Jesus Do?" It's a great reminder for all of us to think about how we should act.

- Talk to God and ask for help: DEAR GOD, I WANT TO NOTICE PEOPLE AROUND ME WHO DON'T QUITE FIT IN. PLEASE GIVE ME COURAGE TO FIND A WAY TO INCLUDE THEM AND SHOW THEM YOUR LOVE. AMEN.

- Seek out someone in your life who may be different in some way and perhaps feels excluded. Do something to include that person. Maybe ask her to sit with you at lunch or start a conversation about her favorite book, game, or show. Be genuine and have the courage to follow through if you start a new friendship.

TAKE IT FURTHER

You can read about Jesus calling the twelve disciples and explore the courage they had to say yes in "The Called" in *The Action Bible* or read Luke 6:12–16.

JONAH & FISH

WHEN LIFE FEELS SO HARD

"I HAVE TOLD YOU THESE THINGS, SO THAT IN ME YOU MAY HAVE PEACE. IN THIS WORLD YOU WILL HAVE TROUBLE. BUT TAKE HEART! I HAVE OVERCOME THE WORLD."

JOHN 16:33

Jose was going through a difficult time. He trusted God that things would get better, but his sadness about some things going on with friends at church, his team, and his grandma was building. He had talked to his leader at church who reminded him that life can be hard and weigh us down. His leader assured Jose that sadness is a normal thing everyone deals with at some point.

With strength you can stay close to God when bad things happen. There was a person in the Bible who dealt with a lot of sadness and suffering, and we can look to him as an example of courage and faith.

The Old Testament tells us about Job, a faithful man who loved God. Satan came to God and said Job was only good because God protected him and gave him everything he had. God said that wasn't true. Job was a true believer who loved Him. He allowed Satan to take away all the good things in Job's life to show that Job had great faith and would always be devoted to God. Job greatly suffered. But as low as his life became, he refused to turn from God. Satan took away Job's family and business and even filled his body with sickness and sores. Still, Job wouldn't turn from God.

There will always be hard times in this world, but God wants us to trust in His care for us.

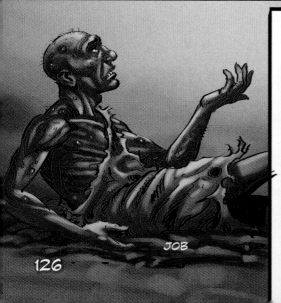

JOB

DISCIPLES IN STORM

- A good way to break up feelings of sadness is to think of things that bring you joy. Close your eyes and think about three things that make you happy. Open your eyes. Did that make you smile? That's just one easy way to feel better when you're sad. When sadness doesn't leave our hearts, it can become something more serious called depression. It's important to talk to an adult if you have a sadness that won't go away.

- Tell God how you're feeling: DEAR GOD, THANK YOU FOR SENDING JESUS TO THIS WORLD TO SAVE ME. I KNOW THAT YOU'RE WITH ME IN EVERY MOMENT—THE GOOD TIMES AND THE BAD TIMES. PLEASE GIVE ME COURAGE TO STAY STRONG WHEN I'M FEELING DOWN. AMEN.

- Go outside and take a walk or just sit and listen. Notice all the parts of nature. God created it and called it good. If He delights in His creation, He surely delights in you and who He created you to be. Spend time enjoying nature and look for God's peace in its beauty.

TAKE IT FURTHER

You can read about Job's story in "God's Wager" in *The Action Bible* or in the book of Job. Read Zechariah 10:12 for further encouragement.

DAVID & GOLIATH

FEELING GOD'S STREAM OF GRACE

THEREFORE, SINCE WE HAVE BEEN JUSTIFIED THROUGH FAITH, WE HAVE PEACE WITH GOD THROUGH OUR LORD JESUS CHRIST, THROUGH WHOM WE HAVE GAINED ACCESS BY FAITH INTO THIS GRACE IN WHICH WE NOW STAND.

ROMANS 5:1–2

Have you ever been out in nature, maybe on a hike with your family, and found a beautiful stream? You take off your shoes and dip your feet into the crystal-clear water. It's cold as ice, fresh and crisp and sparkling. You can feel little pebbles and sand beneath your feet, and you look for little minnows swimming by. You feel the hot sun shining down on you, and you smile as you stand in the stream, happy to be in the beautiful world God created.

Romans talks about God's grace like someone standing in a sparkling stream. Because Jesus died on the cross for our sins and then rose from the grave, when we believe in Him by faith, God's grace saves us. God's grace is His favor that we did nothing to earn; He offers it to us. We stand in this grace and it feels as refreshing and new as standing in a stream. We're drenched in it. It flows all around us and covers over all our sins. What amazing grace God has shown to us!

ANGEL & MARY

MIRIAM

God loved the world so much that He sent His own Son to die for us. When you accept Jesus, His sacrifice stands in place of all your sin. There is peace between you and God, and He places you in His streams of grace.

- When you read the Bible, it becomes clear how much God loves you. He died for you, He chose you, and He saved you. And what's amazing is that He did the same for every other believer too. Whenever you feel sad or worried or scared, know God loves you so much that He sent Jesus to cover you in His grace.

- Take time to tell God how thankful you are: DEAR GOD, THANK YOU FOR YOUR GREAT LOVE! THANK YOU FOR BLESSING ME WITH YOUR GRACE. HELP ME TO LIVE EACH DAY FOR YOU, AND TO LOVE YOU AND THOSE AROUND ME. AMEN.

- Consider drawing a picture of yourself standing in a stream of water. If you don't like to draw, take a picture of yourself in a stream or write a story about it. Let your finished work remind you of God's grace that flows around you because of what Jesus did for you.

TAKE IT FURTHER

The apostle Paul wrote many letters about God's grace. Check out "Prison Pen Pals" in *The Action Bible* or read the book of Ephesians to discover more about what Paul wrote.

ESTHER & KING XERXES

WHEN YOU'RE FEELING HOPELESS

IN THE SAME WAY, THE SPIRIT HELPS US IN OUR WEAKNESS. WE DO NOT KNOW WHAT WE OUGHT TO PRAY FOR, BUT THE SPIRIT HIMSELF INTERCEDES FOR US THROUGH WORDLESS GROANS.

ROMANS 8:26

Have you ever gone from really good feelings to really bad feelings in a short amount of time? Goal scored; goal gets taken away. New kitten; kitten gets sick. Flying down the hill on your bike; arm gets broken. It can be jarring to swing from a high to a low. A man in the Bible had that happen to him, and it was hard for him to understand.

During Elijah's time, things were out of control with people worshipping all kinds of idols. God guided Elijah, His prophet, to put an end to the craziness. Queen Jezebel found out about this and she didn't like it one bit. She sent someone to threaten Elijah, and he fled for his life and hid in the wilderness. In his distress, Elijah told God he was done and wanted to die.

Elijah was as low as he could be, wanting to end his own life. However, God was with him and provided for him. An angel came and touched Elijah and brought food and drink. After Elijah regained his strength, he traveled to Mount Horeb,

DISCIPLES

JONATHAN

known as God's mountain. There Elijah experienced the presence of the Lord as He passed by. Don't ever forget that God is always with you!

- Even at his lowest point, Elijah talked to God. Elijah stood on top of one of the holiest mountains in the presence of God because God infused strength into him when he didn't even want to live. God can give you that hope too. Just ask and accept it—in whatever form it comes.

- Here's a way you can pray: HOLY SPIRIT, WHEN I AM WEAK, I DON'T KNOW THE RIGHT WORDS TO PRAY. YOU KNOW EVERYTHING I'M GOING THROUGH. I'M GLAD YOU ARE ALWAYS WITH ME AND KNOW WHAT I NEED. AMEN.

- Sometimes life can seem hopeless. Remember to never give up. God is always with you and He is always there to listen. It's important to also talk to a trusted friend or adult if you're having serious thoughts about harming yourself in any way.

TAKE IT FURTHER

You can read the story of Elijah in "The Sound of Silence" in *The Action Bible* or in 1 Kings 19. Jeremiah 29:11 is a wonderful verse that shares of the hope we have in knowing that God has a plan for us.

MARY, JOSEPH, & JESUS TO EGYPT.

WHEN TO BE DIFFERENT

*DO NOT CONFORM TO THE PATTERN OF THIS WORLD, BUT
BE TRANSFORMED BY THE RENEWING OF YOUR MIND. THEN
YOU WILL BE ABLE TO TEST AND APPROVE WHAT GOD'S
WILL IS—HIS GOOD, PLEASING AND PERFECT WILL.*

ROMANS 12:2

God created you in His image to be … you! He wants you to think for yourself and to make decisions that honor Him. As you learn, develop, and grow your mind, you discover more about how *His* mind works. He is always with you, even when you are in class, reading, or doing schoolwork. As you get older, you will have choices to make each day. When you decide to follow Jesus with the way you live your life, you will often have to make choices that will set you apart from others. You may end up talking, acting, or dressing differently from kids around you. That's better than being mindlessly pulled along by what the rest of the world is doing, because they often don't think about Jesus at all. God cares how you talk to a friend, pick out your clothes, or look at things online.

John the Baptist was a unique person who certainly didn't "go along." He was a strong leader who paved the way for Jesus' ministry. John wasn't typical; he wore clothes made out of camel's hair and ate bugs (see Matthew 3:4). Many people came to John to hear him speak of the coming Savior and to be baptized in the Jordan River. John even baptized Jesus! John was a special leader who cared most about being in God's will.

ZACCHAEUS
& JESUS

KING DAVID
& ABIGAIL

- The world needs people who are set apart by their desire to follow Jesus. Be thoughtful and seek God's guidance through prayer, quiet time, and listening to Him. Lead with strength of character. Educate yourself, take time to get to know the leaders in your life and what they stand for, treat others well, and use your strong mind to make the best decisions for yourself.

- A prayer for leaders: DEAR GOD, GIVE ME STRENGTH TO LEAD WELL AND MAKE GOOD CHOICES IN YOUR NAME. AMEN. A prayer for followers: DEAR GOD, HELP ME SUPPORT OTHERS WITH STRENGTH, ALWAYS BLESSING YOUR NAME. AMEN.

- The next time you sit down to eat, start a conversation about good ways to be different from everything you see around you. What is good different? Bad different? Start each morning by inviting God into your day as you learn, think, and process new things. Ask Him to use each day to show you when to lead and when to follow.

TAKE IT FURTHER

For more about John the Baptist, read "Baptized" in *The Action Bible* or Matthew 3.

JOHN THE BAPTIST & JESUS

WHEN YOU WANT TO QUIT THE RACE

LET US THROW OFF EVERYTHING THAT HINDERS AND THE SIN THAT SO EASILY ENTANGLES. AND LET US RUN WITH PERSEVERANCE THE RACE MARKED OUT FOR US, FIXING OUR EYES ON JESUS, THE PIONEER AND PERFECTER OF FAITH. FOR THE JOY SET BEFORE HIM HE ENDURED THE CROSS, SCORNING ITS SHAME, AND SAT DOWN AT THE RIGHT HAND OF THE THRONE OF GOD.

HEBREWS 12:1-2

Jessie hated the mile run in PE class. She liked sprints; she was good at sprints. Give her a fast, short run any day. But the mile—ugh! Playing tag during recess was a little different, but the organized races were so hard for some reason. The PE coach tried to offer some advice: "When you sprint in a short race, you can see the end in sight and that might encourage you to have strength to run strong and finish well. With a longer race, you have to pace yourself to make it to the finish line."

The words in the verses above are to encourage and remind followers of Jesus to think of life like a race. You're going to have to make good choices in how you run the race in order to make it to the finish line. Ask Jesus for courage and

JACOB & ISAAC

TIMOTHY

strength to persevere, to get through, hard times. Remember that Jesus faced the ultimate challenge when He was crucified for all the sins of humanity.

- When Jesus died on the cross, He made the way for God to forgive anyone who asks for forgiveness—including you! As you choose to live a strong life of faith, remember Jesus' story and the sacrifice He made for you. When you make choices each day, ask yourself: How would Jesus want me to react to this? When you feel like you've run away from Jesus, He is waiting close by. You can reach out to Him in prayer.

- Pray this prayer: CREATOR GOD, YOU MADE ME AND YOU HAVE A PATH MARKED OUT FOR MY RACE. WHEN I GET TIRED OF DOING THE RIGHT THING, PLEASE REMIND ME THAT YOU ARE WITH ME. YOU GIVE ME STRENGTH TO PERSEVERE AND I TRUST YOU, EVEN WHEN I FEEL TIRED. AMEN.

- It's time for a run! Lace up your gym shoes and grab a friend or your family. Take a jog around your neighborhood or head to a track at a local high school. As you run, pay attention to everything around you. Think about the race God has set for you and talk to Him about staying strong.

TAKE IT FURTHER

You can read about the book of Hebrews in "The Final Letters" in *The Action Bible*. For further encouragement about running with God, read 1 Corinthians 9:24.

SAMARITAN WOMAN
& JESUS

WHEN YOU SLOW YOUR ANGER

Erica had been working hard to set up her grandmother's antique dollhouse. She'd spent painstaking hours repairing tiny wooden furniture and arranging miniature cups and plates and utensils in the kitchen. One day when she returned from school, she found everything inside the dollhouse a jumbled mess. Erica assumed her toddler sister, Caitlin, had come into her room and "played" with her dollhouse. She yelled for her little sister in anger just as her mom quickly came into the room. Mom explained that she had accidentally bumped the dollhouse while vacuuming and everything had jostled. She apologized and told Erica that Caitlin had nothing to do with it. Erica was still disappointed at how things looked, but she realized it would have been better to ask than to instantly get angry and assume the worst.

James wrote the words in the verse above as advice he sent out to followers of Christ. The entire first chapter of the book of James is full of helpful reminders on how to live and serve with love, patience, and respect for others.

ESAU

LEAH & RACHEL

- Has a sibling, cousin, or friend ever pushed you to the very limit of your patience? Did you blow up in anger and frustration? How could Erica have handled the situation differently? Maybe she could have spent some time looking more closely at the dollhouse to see whether things were just out of place or really ruined. Or maybe she could have felt sad for a little bit and then asked her mom or dad to help her fix the arrangement. You always have choices to control your anger and seek patience.

- God hears your prayers: DEAR GOD, I ADMIT THAT I HAVE LOST MY TEMPER AND GOTTEN ANGRY QUICKLY. PLEASE FORGIVE ME FOR THE TIME WHEN I ... PLEASE GIVE ME PATIENCE SO I CAN SLOW DOWN, BE A BETTER LISTENER, AND SHOW LOVE. AMEN.

- Seek out someone you may have recently lost your temper with. Invite that person to play a game with you, ride bikes, or walk your dog together. It's never too late to say you're sorry and move forward doing the right thing.

TAKE IT FURTHER

Read more about James in "The Final Letters" in *The Action Bible*. For more encouragement in seeking patience when you're feeling angry, read Ephesians 4:26; Numbers 14:18; and Colossians 3:8.

JESUS & BOY WITH LUNCH

WHEN COMPLAINING COMES NATURALLY

*THE LORD SAID TO MOSES, "I HAVE HEARD THE
GRUMBLING OF THE ISRAELITES."*

EXODUS 16:11-12

Josh and his mom were almost home when she casually mentioned one more stop they needed to make. "But Mom!" he whined. "We haven't been home all day, and I need to work on my model!" His mom pulled into the grocery store parking lot. "Remember this morning when you complained about us being out of milk? That's why we're stopping."

The Israelites were God's people—the people He had just rescued from slavery in Egypt. Just before the grumbling in these verses above, God had sent hail from the sky, frogs from the river, locusts to eat crops, and turned the sky dark for days. God had even split the Red Sea so His people could cross over on dry land. He had performed these miracles to show the Israelites His power so they would know they could trust Him. And yet here the Israelites were, a few days later, complaining because they were hungry and didn't trust that God was going to provide.

It's easy to read about the complaining Israelites and roll our eyes. But we're not so different from the Israelites. God has provided so much for us—food, clothes, family, friends, school, the list goes on. And most importantly, He sent Jesus to die on the cross for our sins and provide us with salvation. And yet, we often have complaining spirits. We don't trust God to help us and provide.

JESUS, MARY,
& MARTHA

JOSHUA &
PROMISED LAND

God has shown us over and over that He is faithful and can be trusted, no matter what. Instead of complaining or worrying, we can turn to Him and ask for His guidance.

- Think back through your past week. Where did you trust God? Where did you complain? Oftentimes, complaining becomes a habit because you aren't grateful for how God has provided for you. Break the habit! Thank God for your parents, friends, and siblings rather than wanting to change them. When you stop to be thankful, it can change your attitude in a minute!

- Close your eyes and talk to God: DEAR GOD, IT'S SO EASY FOR ME TO COMPLAIN. REMIND ME OF ALL I HAVE TO BE THANKFUL FOR AND HELP ME TO TRUST YOU WITH EVERYTHING GOING ON IN MY LIFE. AMEN.

- Over the next few days, try to catch yourself when you begin to complain. Instead, be grateful and see how you can bring joy (by helping, by smiling, by saying something kind) to the situation instead.

TAKE IT FURTHER

You can read the story of the Israelites in "The Complaining Begins" in *The Action Bible* or read Exodus 15–17. Ephesians 4:29–32 has a lot of great advice for how we should talk and how to remember to be grateful for what Jesus has done in our lives.

MARY & JESUS

JESUS & LAZARUS

WHO ARE YOU FOLLOWING?

IN THOSE DAYS ISRAEL HAD NO KING; EVERYONE DID AS THEY SAW FIT.

JUDGES 21:25

Have you ever heard an older person say something like, "When I was a kid, people didn't behave like they do now"? This may be true. Or maybe we just see more of the bad now that we have constant access to the internet and social media. It's so easy to know what's wrong in our world today.

The truth is that every culture in history has been sinful because they've been filled with sinful people. When we abandon God and don't follow Him, we fail at life in many ways. Even cultures that acknowledge God have often twisted the Bible to get away with terrible things like slavery or mistreating others.

This is what happened to Israel in the book of Judges. Things went from bad to worse for God's people. They weren't following God, and without Him to lead and guide them everyone did whatever they wanted. It happened back in Bible times, and it will keep happening until Jesus returns.

The good news is that we *do* have a king—Jesus—and He loves us, died for us, and sends us His Holy Spirit to show us how to live for Him, even when the people around us are doing whatever they want.

JESUS & DISCIPLES

JESUS ON DONKEY

- Do you have friends who don't care about what is right or true? The pressure makes it hard to stand out and be different from our friends. This is where faith comes in. Although it's not easy to follow Jesus, He promises to be with us and to help us. And if we have faith in His way and His Word, it's worth it to follow Him no matter what.

- You can talk to God anytime: DEAR GOD, GIVE ME THE COURAGE TO BE DIFFERENT FROM THOSE AROUND ME IF THEY DON'T FOLLOW YOUR WAYS. GIVE ME FAITH TO LOVE OTHERS. AMEN.

- Think of a way this week that you can stand out for Jesus. This could mean not participating in an unkind conversation or standing up for what you believe in a discussion. Whatever it is, ask God to give you the strength and faith to claim Him as your King! Share what happens around the dinner table.

TAKE IT FURTHER

You can read more about this time in Israel in "Left-Handed Judge" in *The Action Bible* or read Psalm 1. Think about the difference between those who do what is right in their own eyes and those who walk in God's way.

JEZEBEL & ELIJAH

PETER & JESUS

FOR SUCH A TIME AS THIS

"FOR IF YOU REMAIN SILENT AT THIS TIME, RELIEF AND DELIVERANCE FOR THE JEWS WILL ARISE FROM ANOTHER PLACE, BUT YOU AND YOUR FATHER'S FAMILY WILL PERISH. AND WHO KNOWS BUT THAT YOU HAVE COME TO YOUR ROYAL POSITION FOR SUCH A TIME AS THIS?"

ESTHER 4:14

Sometimes Cole felt like God was nowhere to be found. Cole's life had been hard, like when he lost his dad to cancer when he was little. Why did he have to grow up without a father? And then his mom had to deal with things all by herself.

When we struggle with hard things in life, such as disappointment, depression, or confusion, we might wonder why God doesn't do more to make things right. But He is always at work, often in ways we can't know, putting things in place so we can make a choice that honors Him at just the right time. Although things may not be easy for you, God might be planning to use you in a special way right where He has you or shaping you through your unique experiences.

This is what God was doing in Esther's life. Although God is never directly mentioned when you read Esther's story, He is at work behind the scenes. Esther was a young Jewish girl who unexpectedly became queen. Later she found out there was a plot to kill all the Jewish people. She was forced to ask herself if she should use her position to convince the king to save her people.

This question was serious. Esther could face death for speaking up to the king when he hadn't asked her to. But her cousin, Mordecai, reminded her that maybe she had been given her position as queen for this exact time.

SAUL & SAMUEL

ANGEL & JACOB

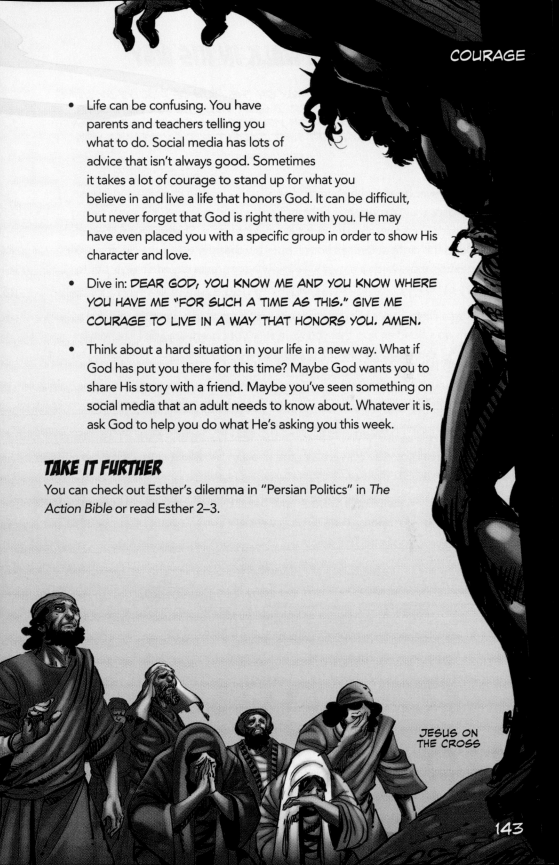

- Life can be confusing. You have parents and teachers telling you what to do. Social media has lots of advice that isn't always good. Sometimes it takes a lot of courage to stand up for what you believe in and live a life that honors God. It can be difficult, but never forget that God is right there with you. He may have even placed you with a specific group in order to show His character and love.

- Dive in: DEAR GOD, YOU KNOW ME AND YOU KNOW WHERE YOU HAVE ME "FOR SUCH A TIME AS THIS." GIVE ME COURAGE TO LIVE IN A WAY THAT HONORS YOU. AMEN.

- Think about a hard situation in your life in a new way. What if God has put you there for this time? Maybe God wants you to share His story with a friend. Maybe you've seen something on social media that an adult needs to know about. Whatever it is, ask God to help you do what He's asking you this week.

TAKE IT FURTHER

You can check out Esther's dilemma in "Persian Politics" in *The Action Bible* or read Esther 2–3.

JESUS ON
THE CROSS

143

WHEN YOU WALK IN HIS WAY

Have you ever been somewhere and needed to make a choice—and it was pretty clear that one way was right and one way was wrong? Kylie was facing that choice right now and she didn't like the pressure. She had been so excited to spend the night at Reese's house, but now that she was there Reese was suggesting they watch a movie Kylie knew her parents wouldn't allow her to watch. Kylie didn't want to disappoint Reese, but she knew it wouldn't be right.

We all face choices like this all the time. Perhaps your brother told you to download an app that you were sure your mom wouldn't like. Maybe everyone decided to ignore the new boy at school. Whenever you get that little prick in your gut—something that makes you a bit uncomfortable because you've been taught that certain choices are wrong—you know what you *should* do.

The Bible tells us the best way to make the right choice is to know God's Word and then live by it. It's how we stay pure or clean before God—we do what He tells us to.

If you've hidden God's Word in your heart by memorizing parts of it or reading it, then when you have a choice to make you'll be sensitive to

BOY JESUS
IN TEMPLE

God reminding you of what the Bible says and how to live for Him.

- You will always face peer pressure and have to decide whether to do the right thing. Kids, teenagers, and adults face it. It never goes away! But knowing God's Word helps us to live with integrity (meaning honesty and consistency). God's Word can shape us into people who not only know what it says but also do what it says.

- You could tell God this: DEAR GOD, I KNOW YOU'VE GIVEN ME THE BIBLE SO I CAN KNOW YOUR STORY AND THE TRUTH. HELP ME HIDE IT IN MY HEART AND MAKE CHOICES THAT LET ME LIVE WITH INTEGRITY. AMEN.

- Have you made a choice recently that didn't honor God? Take time to make it right. First ask God to forgive you—and He will! Then if there is someone you need to apologize to, go see them. Consider learning a verse to remind you of the choice God wants you to make.

TAKE IT FURTHER

When Jesus was tempted to sin, He quoted Scripture and made the right choice. See "Tempted in the Desert" in *The Action Bible* or in Luke 4:1–13.

JOSEPH & BROTHERS

ADAM & EVE

145

WHEN YOU GIVE IT OVER TO GOD

*COMMIT TO THE LORD WHATEVER YOU DO, AND
HE WILL ESTABLISH YOUR PLANS.*

PROVERBS 16:3

There went his plans for the weekend! Brett was going to spend the night at his good friend's house and then they were going to help with the church service project. But that all depended on Brett's vocabulary test grade. He thought he was going to do great on it, but despite all his studying he failed! Now he was grounded and was going to have to stay home and study extra hard for the next test.

Most of us like to make plans and have things to look forward to. They may be short-term, such as dinner tonight or a game next week. Or they may be long-term, such as the car you hope to own years from now. The Bible reminds us that it's important to share our desires with God in a way that recognizes He is the one in charge.

When we talk to God about the future, we can tell Him what we're hoping for and that we realize He knows what is best for us. Committing what we do to the Lord really just means that we trust Him with our plans, our hopes, and our goals.

NAAMAN &
SERVANT GIRL

146

- Things can change in life. You may have thought you'd always live in the same house, and then suddenly your parents decide to move. Your ideas about how things should be may disappear. This uncertainty can be frustrating, so remember to take it to God. He is unchanging and will guide you through difficulties with the Bible and His Holy Spirit.

- Here's what you can pray: DEAR GOD, HELP ME TO COME TO YOU WITH ANYTHING. I PRAY YOU WILL GUIDE MY HOPES AND DREAMS AND DECISIONS. I WANT TO FOLLOW YOU AND WHAT YOU HAVE PREPARED FOR ME. THANK YOU FOR LOVING ME! AMEN.

- What do you have coming up this week on your calendar? Are they fun things or worrying things? Add prayer reminders to your calendar. Give them to God. He is in control. Ask for a heart that listens for guidance!

TAKE IT FURTHER

Explore the winding story of Joseph's life beginning with "Big Dreams" in *The Action Bible* or in Genesis 37. See what God did in Joseph's life, which was very different from what Joseph expected!

JESUS & BLIND MAN

NOAH & ANIMALS

FEELING THE JOY OF HONESTY

*DECEIT IS IN THE HEARTS OF THOSE WHO PLOT EVIL,
BUT THOSE WHO PROMOTE PEACE HAVE JOY.*
PROVERBS 12:20

Tess didn't feel right about it as she walked away from her friends. Why had she just told that lie? In trying to fit in, she had exaggerated what she did this summer so people would think she was more interesting. She wanted to be liked so much! But feeling like this now wasn't worth it. How was she going to keep up with that lie? And when her friends found out, they would be hurt.

Have you ever caught someone in a lie? It may have been when a younger sibling blamed you for something she actually did. Or maybe one of your friends at school spread a false rumor. When someone lies—even if it's not about you—how does it make you feel? Hurt, frustrated, angry, confused?

The Bible tells us that deceit is an evil action. Lying creates chaos and hurt feelings, and it takes away trust. When we live truthful, peaceful lives, joy comes with it!

JOSHUA & WALL
OF JERICHO

PRODIGAL SON
& FATHER

- The temptation to lie or distort the truth can be strong. With the continual comparison in the world and on social media, you want to appear better to others. You may even share something dishonest to hurt someone else. But the Bible says that when you live a life of integrity and honesty, you will have more joy. It's freeing when you aren't hiding secrets or keeping track of lies.

- Pray this prayer: DEAR GOD, PLEASE FORGIVE ME FOR THE LIES I'VE TOLD. THANK YOU FOR ALWAYS FORGIVING ME. HOLY SPIRIT, HELP ME TO BE SOMEONE OTHERS CAN TRUST TO TELL THE TRUTH. AMEN.

- Is there someone you've lied to or about? Ask God to give you the strength and courage to say you're sorry. It's never too late to start living a fresh way. Consider writing down Proverbs 12:20 and placing it in your Bible as a reminder that integrity brings joy!

TAKE IT FURTHER

The very first lie happened in the garden of Eden when the serpent lied to Eve. Read about it in "Tempted in the Garden" in *The Action Bible* or in Genesis 2.

ABRAHAM, SARAH, & ISAAC

WHEN YOU CHOOSE KINDNESS

A GENTLE ANSWER TURNS AWAY WRATH, BUT A HARSH WORD STIRS UP ANGER.

PROVERBS 15:1

When Harper posted the picture of her new hairstyle, she wasn't prepared for the comments she received online. Some were kind, but others were downright mean! Her gut reaction was to respond with similar comments and defend herself. But then she remembered something her grandmother used to say, "If you can't say something nice, don't say anything at all."

It's hard to live by that idea. People argue harshly with one another about pretty much *anything*. And instead of disagreeing in a way that helps people better understand one another, they often do it in a way that makes the situation worse. We can't stop people from saying what's on their minds, but we can control how we respond. If you say something mean to your brother but he responds with sincere kindness or walks away, you'll be less likely to continue being angry or harsh with your words. If someone says something unkind, the Bible tells us that a gentle response can calm the situation.

According to the book of Proverbs in the Bible, getting along with others is the wise way and honors God.

SAMSON & DELILAH

JESUS & HEALED WOMAN

- Sometimes it's difficult to answer people with gentleness. You might feel frustration with those around you. But you can choose to be a calming influence in your discussions so that fights don't get worse. In fact, how you respond may cause those around you to stop and listen to what you have to say.

- Talk to God anytime: DEAR GOD, THANK YOU FOR GIVING ME WISE ADVICE IN YOUR WORD. HELP ME TO CALM SITUATIONS THROUGH GENTLE ANSWERS. THANK YOU FOR YOUR HOLY SPIRIT, WHICH HELPS ME TO GROW TO BE LIKE YOU. AMEN.

- Next time you feel frustrated with someone, take a deep breath and try hard to respond with gentleness instead of harshness. As you answer, notice if it helps change the tone of your conversation. Did the other person become gentler too? Were you able to listen to each other?

TAKE IT FURTHER

For a story that shows a woman who diffused a dangerous situation with kindness, read "A Fool and His Wife …" in *The Action Bible* or read 1 Samuel 25. Read James 1:19–21 for more about the dangers of responding to others with anger.

MOSES & RED SEA

151

ON THOSE DAYS YOU WANT A FRESH START

*IF YOU, LORD, KEPT A RECORD OF SINS,
LORD, WHO COULD STAND? BUT WITH YOU
THERE IS FORGIVENESS, SO THAT WE
CAN, WITH REVERENCE, SERVE YOU.*

PSALM 130:3-4

Brayden's mom said he had a memory like an elephant; he remembered every wrong thing people had ever done to him. He recalled the time his sister took his dessert. And the day his mom made him go to school even though he was sick. Oh, and remember the friend who lied about him to a neighbor?

The Bible says that if God kept a record of our sins, the weight of them would crush us. He is God; He knows every little sin we've ever committed. He sees the ones that no one else knows about. Even one sin separates us from God, according to the Bible (see Romans 3:23).

God, however, doesn't keep a record of our sins; instead, He is always willing to forgive us when we come to Him and turn from our sin. There is nothing we can do that God won't forgive us for. He forgives our sins and then doesn't hold them against us. He forgives us so we can start living for Him again. What an amazing God we serve!

PAUL & BLINDING LIGHT

DEBORAH & BARAK

- God knows we'll never be good enough on our own, which is why He sent Jesus to die in our place. He took all of our sins on Himself, and when we accept what He's done for us God wipes away our sin and replaces it with righteousness! When we are in relationship with God and recognize how incredible He is, we serve Him. We serve God by making choices that honor Him, turning from sin and asking for forgiveness when we don't, and loving and serving those around us.

- You could pray like this: DEAR GOD, I CONFESS MY SINS TO YOU. THANK YOU FOR SENDING JESUS TO FORGIVE MY SINS. HELP ME TO LOVE YOU AND LOVE OTHERS IN THE SAME WAY YOU HAVE LOVED ME. AMEN.

- Are there people in your life who have sinned against you and you need to forgive? If God doesn't keep a record of sins, we shouldn't either. Ask God to help you forgive those people, and then make an effort this week to start fresh with them.

TAKE IT FURTHER

You can read the story of Jesus dying on the cross in "Crucified!" in *The Action Bible*. Also read Psalm 103:8–12 as a reminder of how God forgives our sins and takes them away from us.

RAHAB & ISRAELITE SCOUTS

153

WHEN PLANS CHANGE

Do you know what you want to be when you grow up? A police officer? A missionary? A doctor? A teacher? Do you have it all planned out? Most of us, no matter how old we are, have ideas of what we'd like to do in the future. You probably enjoy learning more about your interests through field trips, reading, and camps. But how would you react if God had a different plan for your life? Would you follow God's direction?

This is what King Solomon wanted everyone who read Proverbs 19:21 to think about. God, in His power and sovereignty, has a perfect plan for all His people. The problem is we don't want the same thing that God wants for us. Sometimes we want to do things our way instead.

Throughout the Bible there are stories of people whose lives were changed by God for His purposes. In the Old Testament book of Exodus, Moses told God that he didn't want to be the leader and spokesman for His people. But God had a different plan. Moses ended up bringing the Israelites out of Egypt. In the New Testament book of Acts, a man named Saul acted against the followers of

PAUL'S SHIPWRECK

PHARAOH

Jesus. But God had a different plan. Saul powerfully met with Jesus and his life changed. Saul spread the Gospel all over the world!

Even though God's plan might be unexpected at times, our plan should be to follow God and what He wants for us.

- God uniquely created you. He has given you special abilities and interests. He asks for you to trust Him and follow His powerful plans that He shows you.

- This is a way you can pray: DEAR GOD, THANK YOU FOR MAKING ME WITH UNIQUE HOPES AND DREAMS FOR MY FUTURE. HELP ME SEE WHEN MY DREAMS MIGHT BE DIFFERENT THAN WHAT YOU WANT FOR ME. I WANT TO TRUST YOU AND YOUR PLAN FOR MY LIFE. AMEN.

- Share some of your dreams with a close family member. Work with them to write down some goals on a sheet of paper and place it in your Bible. How will you work toward this goal? How might God shape you along this path?

TAKE IT FURTHER

You can read the story of Moses in "A Burning Bush!" in *The Action Bible*. For more wisdom on God's plans for us, read and memorize Proverbs 16:1.

BOAZ & RUTH
IN FIELD

WHEN YOU'RE FEELING OVERLOOKED

Just one more kennel to scoop and then Alec would be able to go home. He enjoyed his time at the rescue organization after school. People commented on his unending energy, but when it came to other more serious tasks, they didn't always consider him. Sure, it's great to be young, but sometimes people don't value your opinion simply because of your age. Our world doesn't always honor those without positions of power, but God does.

Although we often imagine Jesus' disciples as grown men or dads when they were learning from Jesus, most of them were probably teenagers—not much older than you! These teenage disciples didn't always understand what Jesus was saying or doing. They didn't know that Jesus was going to bring salvation to the world by giving His life. They thought He was going to be a king in Jerusalem and that they would be His top advisers.

But God's kingdom doesn't work the way the world does. When the disciples asked Jesus who was the greatest in the kingdom, He called a child to Him and told the disciples to become more like children. To be great in God's kingdom is to take a lower position—one like a child who is learning and serving and not

DANIEL & LIONS

MARY, JOSEPH, & BABY JESUS

seen as powerful. Jesus' kingdom is upside down from the way the rest of the world works.

- God desires His followers to become more trusting like children and people who serve others. To be a child, or to have a low position, is to have a place of honor in God's kingdom. Jesus invites us to serve Him and others, and He will honor us.

- God hears you when you pray: DEAR GOD, THANK YOU FOR HAVING A KINGDOM THAT LOOKS SO DIFFERENT FROM THE REST OF THE WORLD. HELP ME TO SERVE YOU AND OTHERS WITH CHILDLIKE FAITH. AMEN.

- Think of three ways you can serve others this week. Maybe you can write a note to someone or help your mom with extra chores. Over the next week, take time to serve others. Be open to doing things—show childlike faith and the heart of a servant.

TAKE IT FURTHER

When David was young, he didn't know he was going to be Israel's greatest king. Read about how God chose him while he was still young in "God's New King" from *The Action Bible* or read 1 Samuel 16:1–13.

JONAH & FISH

FOR DAYS OF DISCOURAGEMENT

FOR WHOEVER WANTS TO SAVE THEIR LIFE WILL LOSE IT, BUT WHOEVER LOSES THEIR LIFE FOR ME AND FOR THE GOSPEL WILL SAVE IT. WHAT GOOD IS IT FOR SOMEONE TO GAIN THE WHOLE WORLD, YET FORFEIT THEIR SOUL?

MARK 8:35-36

It was getting uncomfortable on the team bench as the guys' jokes continued to get grosser. Jake kept hoping they would change the subject or the coach would come by and put an end to it. He knew he should step in and ask them to cut it out, but he didn't want to seem too nice. It was hard to admit, but he realized he was sometimes embarrassed to be a Christian.

It isn't always easy to talk about Jesus or to live differently than others, especially when those around you don't share your beliefs. You and your family going to church may set you apart from your friends. Or someone may ask what you believe, and you're ashamed or too scared to tell them about your faith. Jesus knew it would be this way. He told His followers that whoever loses his life for Him will actually save it. We should give up our own will in order to do what Jesus asks of us, knowing that His ways are better. As followers of Jesus, we should be willing to share our faith and to stand out in uncomfortable ways. Jesus is worth it!

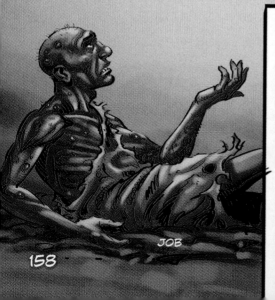

JOB

DISCIPLES IN STORM

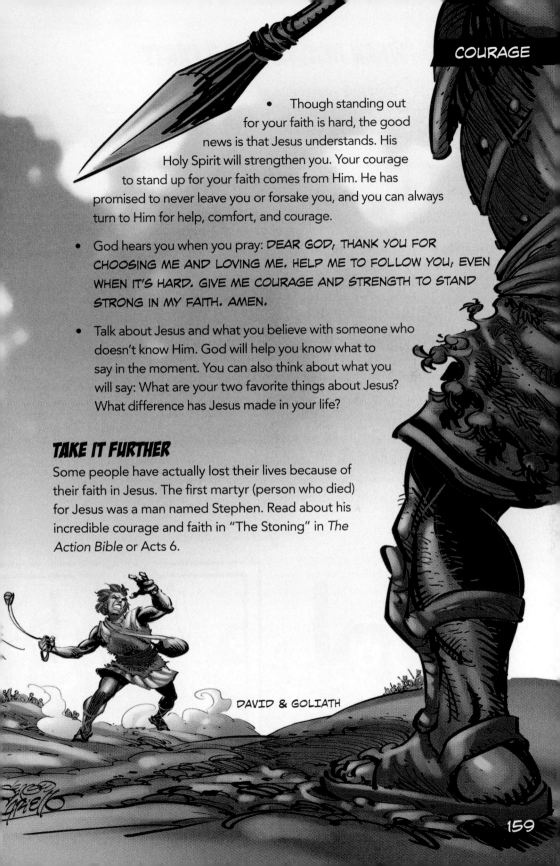

- Though standing out for your faith is hard, the good news is that Jesus understands. His Holy Spirit will strengthen you. Your courage to stand up for your faith comes from Him. He has promised to never leave you or forsake you, and you can always turn to Him for help, comfort, and courage.

- God hears you when you pray: DEAR GOD, THANK YOU FOR CHOOSING ME AND LOVING ME. HELP ME TO FOLLOW YOU, EVEN WHEN IT'S HARD. GIVE ME COURAGE AND STRENGTH TO STAND STRONG IN MY FAITH. AMEN.

- Talk about Jesus and what you believe with someone who doesn't know Him. God will help you know what to say in the moment. You can also think about what you will say: What are your two favorite things about Jesus? What difference has Jesus made in your life?

TAKE IT FURTHER

Some people have actually lost their lives because of their faith in Jesus. The first martyr (person who died) for Jesus was a man named Stephen. Read about his incredible courage and faith in "The Stoning" in *The Action Bible* or Acts 6.

DAVID & GOLIATH

WHEN HEAVEN HAS A PARTY

"'REJOICE WITH ME; I HAVE FOUND MY LOST COIN.' IN THE SAME WAY, I TELL YOU, THERE IS REJOICING IN THE PRESENCE OF THE ANGELS OF GOD OVER ONE SINNER WHO REPENTS."

LUKE 15:9-10

Just one more place to look and then Chris would have to give up. The water bottle itself was nothing that special, but the stickers he had collected on it were from his friends and his travels. He would hate to lose them. He peeked into the dark classroom and there it was! He was so relieved to find it he felt like celebrating.

Have you ever been close to losing something but were able to save or find it in time? Maybe your team made a comeback to win an important game. Or you weren't sure you did well on a difficult test but got the grade you needed. Or you got that part in the play, which was so hard to audition for. Those moments are awesome! It makes you want to celebrate with all your energy. Did you know heaven celebrates when seemingly lost things—people who don't know Jesus—are saved?

Jesus told many parables (or stories) when He taught. One was about a woman who had ten silver coins but lost one. She searched every inch of her house until she found that lost coin. Jesus says it's the same with God and those who don't yet know Him. He looks for and saves the lost and rejoices along with the angels when someone who is lost comes to Him.

ANGEL & MARY

MIRIAM

The Bible tells that all of us are lost in sin before we accept Jesus' gift of salvation. When you decide to follow Jesus, He celebrates along with all of heaven because *you* became a part of His family.

- God calls everyone to know Him, follow Him, and receive His gift of salvation. When you feel lonely or unimportant or scared, remember that Jesus loves you and He wants you!

- Here's a way you can pray: DEAR GOD, THANK YOU FOR SEARCHING FOR ME AND REJOICING OVER ME WHEN I DECIDED TO FOLLOW YOU. HELP ME BE STRONG IN MY FAITH AND TO REMEMBER YOUR GREAT LOVE FOR ME. AMEN.

- We all have people in our lives who don't yet know Jesus as their Savior—family, friends, maybe even people we meet. Start praying for three people who need to know Him. Picture the party that will take place in heaven when those people accept Jesus' gift of salvation!

TAKE IT FURTHER

You can read more about the lost being found in "Lost and Found" in *The Action Bible* or read Luke 15.

ESTHER &
KING XERXES

WHEN HOPE SEEMS LOST

"WHY DO YOU LOOK FOR THE LIVING AMONG THE DEAD? HE IS NOT HERE; HE HAS RISEN! REMEMBER HOW HE TOLD YOU, WHILE HE WAS STILL WITH YOU IN GALILEE: 'THE SON OF MAN MUST BE DELIVERED OVER TO THE HANDS OF SINNERS, BE CRUCIFIED AND ON THE THIRD DAY BE RAISED AGAIN.'"

LUKE 24:5-7

Have you ever had a day that seemed entirely hopeless? Maybe you fought with your friend and didn't know how you would ever fix things. Or your parents said they didn't have enough money to buy groceries. Or you couldn't explain why but you felt so sad that you just didn't care about anything. That's how the women felt the day they went to the tomb.

Back when Jesus lived, women weren't always treated fairly. But God created both men and women in His image. The very first people to hear about Jesus rising from the dead were women! They had gone to Jesus' tomb after He died to care for His body. Imagine their shock when, instead of seeing Jesus, they met bright, shining men who told them that Jesus had risen from the dead!

Jesus told His disciples many times He had to die, and He would rise again three days later. But no one quite understood it until it happened. The women, when they heard from the angels, suddenly remembered Jesus' words. The Messiah they thought had died was actually alive and well—God had done something

DISCIPLES

JONATHAN

amazing that was about to change the entire world! This gift of salvation brought the disciples new hope.

- The women thought all their hopes died with Jesus. But they discovered an amazing miracle that day—God raised Jesus from the dead! With Jesus, we are never without hope. He beat death and He is with us. He gives us hope for each day.

- God hears you when you pray: DEAR GOD, THANK YOU SO MUCH FOR HOPE. I HAVE HOPE TO BE SAVED, HOPE FOR MY LIFE, AND HOPE FOR EACH DAY. HELP ME TO SHARE YOUR PROMISE WITH OTHERS. AMEN.

- On a piece of paper, write the word HOPE in big, bubble letters. In each of those letters write down words or situations or memories that bring you hope. Hang it on your wall or put it in your Bible as a reminder of the hope Jesus brings.

TAKE IT FURTHER

Read about the women discovering Jesus had risen from the dead in "The Sealed Tomb" in *The Action Bible* or read John 20:1–18.

MARY, JOSEPH, & JESUS TO EGYPT.

FOR TIMES WHEN YOU NEED A GUIDE

AND I WILL ASK THE FATHER, AND HE WILL GIVE
YOU ANOTHER ADVOCATE TO HELP YOU AND BE
WITH YOU FOREVER—THE SPIRIT OF TRUTH.

JOHN 14:16-17

Chad approached the group of older boys gathered behind the tree on the playground. They were looking at something. As he got closer, he had a weird feeling about it. They were looking at some bad videos on someone's phone. Chad knew he shouldn't participate so he turned around and walked away.

Do you ever get a strong feeling telling you to get away from something or someone? Or do you ever feel lonely or scared or unsure of what to do? The Bible tells us that when we become Christians, Jesus sends the Holy Spirit to live with us. He helps us, comforts us, and guides us in truth.

The Holy Spirit has always existed, just like God and Jesus have. He is the third person of the Trinity. Although the Spirit might be a little hard to understand, He is just as important as God and Jesus. When we trust Him, He helps us to be kind, loving, joyful, peaceful, self-controlled, and so much more. In the Old Testament He even filled men with wisdom, understanding, and skills so they could design beautiful artwork for the tabernacle and all the things

ZACCHAEUS
& JESUS

KING DAVID
& ABIGAIL

that would go into it! God's Spirit lives within us and helps us.

- When you are a Christian, Jesus sends the Holy Spirit to live with you and to help you. When you call on Him and trust Him, He will guide you. When you're not sure if you should gossip with your friends, the Holy Spirit will remind you of what is true and right. When you're feeling scared, ask the Holy Spirit to fill you with His strength and peace. God gives us His Spirit, and we can depend on Him!

- Take time to talk to God: DEAR GOD, THANK YOU FOR GIVING ME YOUR HOLY SPIRIT TO GUIDE ME AND COMFORT ME. YOU ARE A GOOD GOD, AND I'M THANKFUL THAT YOU CARE ABOUT ME ALL THE TIME. HELP ME TO TRUST YOU EVERY DAY. AMEN.

- Think about the areas in your life where you feel you need help: with friends or schoolwork or controlling your emotions. Read Galatians 5:22–23 and ask the Holy Spirit to fill you with His fruit.

TAKE IT FURTHER

Jesus promised to send the Holy Spirit, but the disciples weren't sure when He would come. Read more of this story in "Waiting for the Spirit" in *The Action Bible* or in Acts 1.

JOHN THE BAPTIST & JESUS

165

WHERE IS GOD'S GOOD PLAN?

AND WE KNOW THAT IN ALL THINGS GOD WORKS FOR THE GOOD OF THOSE WHO LOVE HIM, WHO HAVE BEEN CALLED ACCORDING TO HIS PURPOSE.

ROMANS 8:28

Kat didn't understand why she was having to adjust so much lately. First there was the news of her family's move to a smaller house. Then she had to get rid of half her toys so she could share her room. Now she was being told the whole family had to budget carefully, so there would be no more fun spending. What did that even mean? Why did *everything* have to change?

God has a plan—a good plan. He always has and He always will. From the beginning of the Bible, we see God's plan working its way even through the first sin, choosing a special family in the Israelites and working through them to bring Jesus into the world. God is telling an amazing story about Himself, and He uses people—from Old Testament times all the way until now—in His plans as He shows people what He is like and calls us to Him.

As God brings about His plans, He invites us into what He is doing. And as He does all these things, He works all things together for good. Sometimes this can be hard for us to see. Not everything in our lives is always good or happy or easy. But God's plans are never wrong and never fail. He is in control, and we can trust Him always!

JACOB & ISAAC

TIMOTHY

- As you follow Jesus, you have a chance to help others know Him. You also have the opportunity to trust Jesus no matter what is going on. Sometimes your life will be hard or lonely or frustrating. Jesus never promised that life as a Christian would be easy or happy. But He did promise that He is working all things together for good. Sometimes the best things for us come through something hard. He just may use you to help bring about that good for His glory!

- God hears you when you pray: DEAR GOD, THANK YOU SO MUCH FOR INVITING ME INTO YOUR PLANS! HELP ME TO LIVE FOR YOU AND TO TRUST YOU AS YOU WORK ALL THINGS TOGETHER FOR GOOD. AMEN.

- Think about a situation in your life that was a challenge but something good came out of it. Maybe you had a tough situation with a friend but you learned how to communicate better. Or perhaps your parents had to discipline you but you ended up learning to be more responsible and follow God more closely. God's good work in our lives may not always seem easy, but He uses everything to bring us closer to Him and to advance His plans so that more people know and follow Him!

TAKE IT FURTHER

Joseph learned a lot about how God works good from difficult situations. Read part of his story in "Jailhouse Shock" in *The Action Bible* or in Genesis 39.

SAMARITAN WOMAN
& JESUS

WHEN A WEAKNESS MAKES YOU STRONGER

BUT HE SAID TO ME, "MY GRACE IS SUFFICIENT FOR YOU, FOR
MY POWER IS MADE PERFECT IN WEAKNESS." THEREFORE I
WILL BOAST ALL THE MORE GLADLY ABOUT MY WEAKNESSES,
SO THAT CHRIST'S POWER MAY REST ON ME.

2 CORINTHIANS 12:9

Jessica often prayed and asked God to heal her constant stomachaches. She didn't like this problem with her body that not only hurt but made her feel different from other kids. It was pretty much a disability that kept her from living normally. She knew to ask God to take away something that was causing her sadness or pain.

We all deal with things in life that can be very hard and sad. It might be that your parents fight a lot and you want God to take away their disagreements and bring peace in your house. Or maybe you have pain in your body that causes you daily suffering.

The apostle Paul was one of God's greatest servants. He gave his whole life to telling people about Jesus. Paul could have easily become prideful because he knew that he served God well. But God gave him something—Paul called it a thorn in his flesh—that was a weakness for him. He asked God to take it away, but God reminded him that His grace was enough. We learn that sometimes

ESAU

LEAH & RACHEL

God can use our weaknesses to remind us to always put our hope and trust in Him and not ourselves.

- How can we be grateful for weaknesses or difficulties? Paul reminds us that God can use those things to help us trust Him more. As you think of the situations in your life that you want God to take from you, try to see how God can use your weaknesses to help you depend on Him. What can you learn about God from your troubles? How can you trust Him more?

- When you're feeling weak, pray: DEAR GOD, I KNOW THAT SOMETIMES YOU USE DIFFICULT THINGS TO BRING ME CLOSER TO YOU. HELP ME TRUST YOU WITH MY WEAKNESS AND TRUST YOUR POWER TO WORK IN MY LIFE. AMEN.

- Just because God didn't take away Paul's thorn in his flesh doesn't mean that He won't answer your prayers about the difficult situation in your life. You never need to stop praying for God to change something, but you can trust that He will do whatever is best for His glory and for your good. Whatever you're praying about, ask God to help you trust Him more and more!

TAKE IT FURTHER

Read more about Paul in "The New Paul" in *The Action Bible* or read 2 Corinthians 12.

JESUS & BOY WITH LUNCH

WHEN YOU THINK ABOUT OTHERS

DO NOTHING OUT OF SELFISH AMBITION OR VAIN CONCEIT. RATHER, IN HUMILITY VALUE OTHERS ABOVE YOURSELVES, NOT LOOKING TO YOUR OWN INTERESTS BUT EACH OF YOU TO THE INTERESTS OF THE OTHERS.

PHILIPPIANS 2:3-4

Have you ever heard the story of Snow White? In that fairy tale, the evil queen looks in a mirror each day and asks who is the fairest (or most beautiful) in all the land. The mirror always answers that she is … until one day when it doesn't. She has been replaced by Snow White, who is now the fairest of them all. This makes the vain queen so angry that she focuses all her energy on killing Snow White.

We live in a world where it's easy to become selfish or conceited. It's a natural result of sin for people to look out for themselves. You've probably seen people try to be more popular, funnier, prettier, or feel better about themselves even if it takes putting down others. The message of our world is to get ahead and do whatever is best for you.

But when you enter the family of God, things change. The way Jesus lived was the exact opposite from how the world lives. Jesus served others, loved others, and showed humility. He didn't boast about what He was doing. In fact, He cared

JESUS, MARY, & MARTHA

JOSHUA & PROMISED LAND

so much about other people—including you—that He sacrificed His life on the cross for your sins!

- One of the main things the Bible says makes us more like Jesus is being willing to serve others. Jesus lived a perfect life that represented God's character. He served others all the time. When you put others above yourself, showing humility and love, it will help you grow into a young man or woman of God with Christlike character.

- Finish this prayer silently: DEAR GOD, THANK YOU SO MUCH FOR SENDING YOUR SON WHO SERVED OTHERS. HE EVEN GAVE HIS OWN LIFE! HELP ME BECOME MORE LIKE YOU AS I THINK ABOUT SERVING THOSE AROUND ME BY ... AMEN.

- Who in your life can you serve instead of thinking about your own needs? What could you do? Watch for someone you can serve each day by showing the love of Jesus.

TAKE IT FURTHER

Jesus told a parable about a man who served someone in need, even though no one would have expected him to. Read more about the Good Samaritan in "A Good Neighbor" in *The Action Bible* or read Luke 10:25–37.

MARY & JESUS

JESUS & LAZARUS

WHEN YOU NEED GODLY ADVICE

REJOICE ALWAYS, PRAY CONTINUALLY; GIVE THANKS IN ALL CIRCUMSTANCES; FOR THIS IS GOD'S WILL FOR YOU IN CHRIST JESUS.

1 THESSALONIANS 5:16-18

As Logan prepared to go to a new school, he started to get a little worried. It had been such a fun summer, but now he had to deal with reality again. What would these kids be like? How should he act? Would he always feel this weight of worry? His grandmother, who had taught him about Jesus all his life, pulled out her Bible and turned to 1 Thessalonians. She began to tell him about her favorite verses. They had always given her such practical advice for how to live each day in a way that pleases God.

Throughout your day, no matter what is happening, your goal can be to *rejoice always*. You don't have to be happy with what's going on or pretend to be glad about a situation that's tough. But you can always rejoice because God is good. He has provided you with salvation through Jesus, and He is always in control!

These verses also remind you to *pray continually*. How do you go through your day in prayer? When you wake up, thank God for a new day and rejoice that He has made one! As you talk with friends and interact with your family, pray for God to give you wisdom, kindness, love, and faith. When you get ready for bed, go back through your day. What are you thankful for? Where might you need forgiveness? Talk to God and praise Him for bringing you through another day.

JESUS & DISCIPLES

JESUS ON DONKEY

Give thanks in all circumstances. No matter what is happening in your life, God is in control. He has something to show you about Himself and a way for you to grow closer to Him. The Bible reminds us that God works all things together for good for those who know Him (see Romans 8:28). He is always at work!

- God's desire is for you to live each day rejoicing, praying, and giving thanks. Through the power of the Holy Spirit in your life, you can do these things that honor God and bring you closer to Him.

- Talk to God about how you're feeling right now: DEAR GOD, THANK YOU FOR TELLING ME HOW TO LIVE EACH DAY. GIVE ME COURAGE TO REJOICE AND TO PRAY AND TO BE THANKFUL. AMEN.

- Try it and see the difference! During this next week, practice these three things each day. When your week is over, look back and see how your attitude changed and how you honored the Lord. Tell someone else about it!

TAKE IT FURTHER

Paul and Silas learned to rejoice, pray, and be thankful no matter the circumstances. Read about their time in jail in "Earthquake!" in *The Action Bible* or read Acts 16:19–39.

JEZEBEL & ELIJAH

PETER & JESUS

WHEN YOU KEEP WANTING MORE

BUT GODLINESS WITH CONTENTMENT IS GREAT GAIN. FOR WE BROUGHT NOTHING INTO THE WORLD; AND WE CAN TAKE NOTHING OUT OF IT.
1 TIMOTHY 6:6-7

Mia really liked clothes. It was fun to learn about the latest styles and to be the first one in her class to wear the new trends. She got a thrill leading the other girls in what to wear. But soon after she bought something, she had to get rid of it. That's the thing with fashion—or the latest in gaming or technology. You can't be satisfied with what you have because others are moving on to the next thing.

The trouble with wanting the best, newest thing (or desiring to be sporty or popular or whatever else) is when you can't be content with what you have or with who you are. You may even start to believe that you *deserve* more if you're really faithful to God.

This is what was happening when Paul wrote to Timothy. At the time there were teachers saying that people who were godly would become rich, and others were starting to believe it. But Paul reminded Timothy that being content with what you have is good. When you're born you have nothing, and when you die you'll have nothing. If you're satisfied with having enough food and enough clothing to keep warm, you'll be grateful for how God has provided for you.

SAUL & SAMUEL

ANGEL & JACOB

174

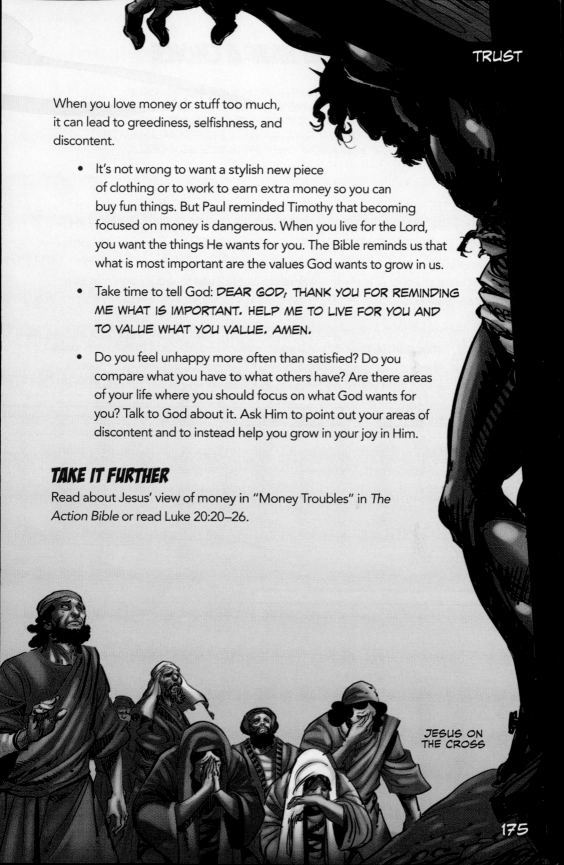

When you love money or stuff too much, it can lead to greediness, selfishness, and discontent.

- It's not wrong to want a stylish new piece of clothing or to work to earn extra money so you can buy fun things. But Paul reminded Timothy that becoming focused on money is dangerous. When you live for the Lord, you want the things He wants for you. The Bible reminds us that what is most important are the values God wants to grow in us.

- Take time to tell God: DEAR GOD, THANK YOU FOR REMINDING ME WHAT IS IMPORTANT. HELP ME TO LIVE FOR YOU AND TO VALUE WHAT YOU VALUE. AMEN.

- Do you feel unhappy more often than satisfied? Do you compare what you have to what others have? Are there areas of your life where you should focus on what God wants for you? Talk to God about it. Ask Him to point out your areas of discontent and to instead help you grow in your joy in Him.

TAKE IT FURTHER

Read about Jesus' view of money in "Money Troubles" in *The Action Bible* or read Luke 20:20–26.

JESUS ON THE CROSS

WHEN YOU HAVE A CHOICE

FLEE THE EVIL DESIRES OF YOUTH AND PURSUE RIGHTEOUSNESS, FAITH, LOVE AND PEACE, ALONG WITH THOSE WHO CALL ON THE LORD OUT OF A PURE HEART. DON'T HAVE ANYTHING TO DO WITH FOOLISH AND STUPID ARGUMENTS, BECAUSE YOU KNOW THEY PRODUCE QUARRELS.

2 TIMOTHY 2:22–23

Kevin and Eli had been riding bikes home from school each day since they met in first grade. Now that they were in sixth grade, they had been growing apart a little bit, but Kevin still cared about Eli. One day they found an unopened bottle of beer lying in the grass. Eli suggested they go home and drink it, but Kevin didn't want any part of it. He knew drinking alcohol was for adults and told Eli to throw it away.

Although you're growing older every day, you're still a young person. It's important to think through your options and ask God to help you make the right choices. Sometimes you'll face peer pressure—your friends might want you to do things that you know you're not supposed to do, and sometimes you may want to follow along. But God asks you to live a life filled with righteousness, making right decisions.

In this part of the Bible, Paul wrote to Timothy to remind him to run away from the evil desires of youth. Everyone struggles with sin their whole lives—young or old. But when you ask God, He will help you turn away from evil and follow Him instead.

BOY JESUS
IN TEMPLE

- No matter what you're thinking about doing, God can help you overcome temptation and instead live in ways that are pleasing to Him. Even though it may be hard, the Holy Spirit can strengthen you. Ask God to help you trust Him. God's desire is that you follow Him and His way because it is the very best way to live!

- God hears you when you call: DEAR GOD, HELP ME AVOID EVIL AND FOLLOW YOU INSTEAD. SHOW ME HOW TO PURSUE YOUR RIGHT LIVING. PLEASE GIVE ME A HEART THAT'S FOR YOU. AMEN.

- Take a minute to list some of the things you see in movies, on social media, or at school that you know are not honoring to God. Now opposite those things, list some activities and things that honor God and help you be faithful and loving. Ask God to give you the power to live with integrity and wisdom.

TAKE IT FURTHER

Josiah became king at eight years old, and from his young age he lived a life that pleased God. You can read his story in "The Boy King of Judah" in *The Action Bible* or read 2 Kings 22.

JOSEPH & BROTHERS

ADAM & EVE

WHEN YOU FEEL LIKE YOU DON'T MEASURE UP

BUT YOU ARE A CHOSEN PEOPLE, A ROYAL PRIESTHOOD, A HOLY NATION, GOD'S SPECIAL POSSESSION, THAT YOU MAY DECLARE THE PRAISES OF HIM WHO CALLED YOU OUT OF DARKNESS INTO HIS WONDERFUL LIGHT.

1 PETER 2:9

Grace and her friends were confused. Often in movies, on TV, or in social media, they heard that everyone is special. But they also got the impression that nothing they did was good enough. They should be thinner, prettier, and smarter.

When you decide to follow Jesus, you become a part of God's chosen people. You belong to Him as His special possession!

Early in the Bible, God chose people to be His very own—the Israelites. He selected them as His treasured possession not because they were anything special, but because He promised to bless the whole world through them.

Hundreds of years later, Jesus was born into a family of Israelites (or Jews, as they were then known). And when Jesus died on the cross and rose from the grave, He invited everyone to join God's family. God kept His promise to bless the whole world through the Israelites because now anyone can become part of God's special family.

God invites you into His family, so that along with the rest of His people you can praise Him for rescuing you from your sin. He brings light to the darkness and He welcomes lonely people into His family. What great love God has shown you!

NAAMAN & SERVANT GIRL

- You have a specific personality, interests, skills, and talents. But the special thing about you is that, along with everyone else, God invites you into His family. When you accept Jesus, He calls you holy and chosen. He wants you to always praise Him for who He is and what He has done. As you grow into who God wants you to be, remember that your identity is found in Jesus and His love.

- You can talk to God anytime: DEAR GOD, THANK YOU FOR INVITING ME INTO YOUR FAMILY AND MAKING ME YOUR SPECIAL TREASURE. HELP ME TO ALWAYS PRAISE YOU AND LIVE SHOWING YOUR LOVE. AMEN.

- On a black piece of construction paper, write the words of 1 Peter 2:9 with white marker or chalk. Memorize it as a way to remember God's love that called you out of darkness and into His light!

TAKE IT FURTHER

You can read about how God's priests served in His magnificent temple in "Solomon's Temple" in *The Action Bible* or read 1 Kings 5–9.

WHEN YOU WANT DIRECTION

GOD SAID TO SOLOMON, "SINCE THIS IS YOUR HEART'S DESIRE AND YOU HAVE NOT ASKED FOR WEALTH, POSSESSIONS OR HONOR, NOR FOR THE DEATH OF YOUR ENEMIES, AND SINCE YOU HAVE NOT ASKED FOR A LONG LIFE BUT FOR WISDOM AND KNOWLEDGE TO GOVERN MY PEOPLE OVER WHOM I HAVE MADE YOU KING, THEREFORE WISDOM AND KNOWLEDGE WILL BE GIVEN YOU."

2 CHRONICLES 1:11-12

Teddy constantly felt like he didn't know what he was doing. Whether it was learning a new kind of math, reading a new piece of music, understanding a new position on his team, or figuring out how to play a new video game, there were so many times when he didn't understand what to do.

As you get older, the only thing that changes are that the decisions and responsibilities get bigger and more important. The feeling of not knowing what to do and needing direction is still there.

Solomon felt the same way. When he was named king of Israel, Solomon was young and didn't know how to lead God's people. So he prayed. Solomon could have asked God for anything—a long life, great power, or more money than he could ever spend—but the young king asked God for wisdom. God answered Solomon's prayer! God blessed him with great wisdom. The Bible describes him as the wisest man who ever lived (see 1 Kings 4:31).

JOSHUA & WALL OF JERICHO

PRODIGAL SON & FATHER

- Solomon's prayer request and God's answer should be a great source of encouragement to you when you face anything you just don't understand. God loves to give wisdom to those who seek it. When you're struggling to understand what to do, in both big and small issues, ask God for wisdom.

- Take time to tell God: DEAR GOD, HELP ME TO ALWAYS SEEK YOUR WISDOM. PLEASE MAKE WISDOM THE DESIRE OF MY HEART MORE THAN MONEY OR THINGS. GIVE ME THE WISDOM TO MAKE GOOD DECISIONS IN ALL AREAS OF MY LIFE. AMEN.

- This week when you're faced with a tough decision at home, in school, on the athletic field, or with your friends, pray and ask God to give you wisdom for your task. It is more valuable to your life than anything else you could pray for God to give you.

TAKE IT FURTHER

You can read some of Solomon's wisdom in "Solomon's Proverbs" in *The Action Bible*. If you want to read more wisdom in God's Word, as recorded by Solomon, check out Proverbs 2:1–15.

ABRAHAM, SARAH, & ISAAC

WHEN YOU NEED POWER IN YOUR LIFE

"THE LORD YOUR GOD DID TO THE JORDAN WHAT HE HAD DONE TO THE RED SEA WHEN HE DRIED IT UP BEFORE US UNTIL WE HAD CROSSED OVER. HE DID THIS SO THAT ALL THE PEOPLES OF THE EARTH MIGHT KNOW THAT THE HAND OF THE LORD IS POWERFUL AND SO THAT YOU MIGHT ALWAYS FEAR THE LORD YOUR GOD."

JOSHUA 4:23-24

Have you ever walked into a river and immediately felt the water rushing past your legs? It's powerful! The current can be so strong, and if you're not careful it can knock you off your feet and carry you away. The powerful current is what carries adventurous people down the river when they go rafting. There is great power in a river—large or small.

In the verses above, the Israelites could see the power of the river's current when they came upon on the banks of the Jordan River. It was flood season, when the river was nearly overflowing with water—so the Jordan was flowing quickly! The Israelites had been carrying the ark of the covenant and came upon the powerful river when God told His people to go and stand in the river. Why? Wouldn't the river's strong current carry away His people and the ark of the covenant?

God is in control and He stopped the flow of the river! God's people took the ark across the river into the land He had promised to them. In His plans, they saw His power on display.

- You may face difficult circumstances that will cause you to wonder if God is powerful enough to help you. Can He help you persevere in learning

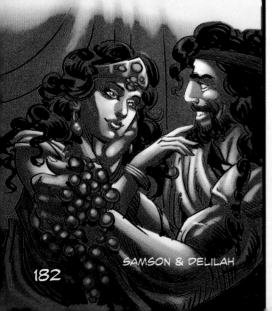

SAMSON & DELILAH

JESUS & HEALED WOMAN

a tough subject? Will He give you the strength to overcome your fears? Just like God showed His power to the Israelites by stopping the rushing water, God can reveal His power through your difficulties. God wants His people to trust Him and His power.

- Close your eyes and talk to God: DEAR GOD, PLEASE HELP ME REMEMBER THAT YOU HAVE THE POWER TO OVERCOME ANYTHING. WHEN THINGS IN MY LIFE ARE CHALLENGING, REMIND ME TO DEPEND ON YOU. AMEN.

- This week, when you face a trouble at home or at school, remember that God has the power you need. Watch for ways to see God's power on display in the world and talk about it with your family. You will gain confidence that He is going to strengthen you.

TAKE IT FURTHER

You can read more about the journey crossing the Jordan River in "Entering the Promised Land" in *The Action Bible* or Joshua 3–4 in the Bible.

MOSES & RED SEA

WHEN YOU NEED THE BEST PATH

WHOEVER WALKS IN INTEGRITY WALKS SECURELY, BUT WHOEVER TAKES CROOKED PATHS WILL BE FOUND OUT.

PROVERBS 10:9

Charlotte was disappointed by what her friend from church was doing. She was fun at church and seemed to know so much about the Bible, but she was acting so differently everywhere else. On the soccer field, she seemed out to hurt other people, she cheated, and she used bad language. Charlotte's parents had taught her to be the same person everywhere.

If you have integrity, people can talk with you and know they can trust your words; friends know they can depend on you. When people see you, they see the real you—not an actor. This is related to your character.

The book of Proverbs is a collection of wisdom given from King Solomon to his son. In the first two chapters of Proverbs, King Solomon emphasizes the importance of being a person who is honest, is trustworthy, and desires to walk in God's ways. This is the straight path, and the one who walks on this path has the peace of walking with good character.

What would make you choose the crooked path? Often it's because you're seeking the approval of others. You want to be liked or to fit in. Sometimes our desire for these things leads us to make choices that go against what we believe.

PAUL & BLINDING LIGHT

DEBORAH & BARAK

- The next time you're trying to fit in, ask yourself if these people will accept you when you walk the straight path in God's ways. If the answer is no, then their friendship is not something you need. The peer pressure that comes when we try to fit in is strong, and it can cause us to choose the crooked path of dishonesty.

- God can help you: DEAR GOD, PLEASE HELP ME TO WALK IN YOUR WAYS. HELP ME NOT TO GIVE IN TO PEER PRESSURE IN ORDER TO FIT IN. GIVE ME THE STRENGTH TO BE A PERSON OF INTEGRITY— EVEN WHEN IT'S HARD. AMEN.

- This week ask a couple of your friends if they see you as a person they can trust. Thank them for their feedback and give God thanks for their friendship. If they cannot trust you, ask them what you can do to earn their trust. Try to memorize Proverbs 10:9 to help you follow it in the way you live your life.

TAKE IT FURTHER

The Bible gives us many examples of what happens when you choose the crooked path. You can read about King Saul and his choices in "Honeycomb Argument" and "The Fall of Saul" in *The Action Bible*, or in 1 Samuel 13–14 and 1 Samuel 26.

RAHAB & ISRAELITE SCOUTS

WHEN YOU HEAR AND BELIEVE

"VERY TRULY I TELL YOU, WHOEVER HEARS MY WORD AND BELIEVES HIM WHO SENT ME HAS ETERNAL LIFE AND WILL NOT BE JUDGED BUT HAS CROSSED OVER FROM DEATH TO LIFE."

JOHN 5:24

Quick … name three things you've heard your parents say again and again. What are a few phrases that made your list? "Clean your room!" "Take care of the dog!" "Get your homework done!" Your parents say these things to you because they want to see action. They want you to hear their words and put them into practice so you can experience the positive outcome of a clean room, a happy pet, or understanding math!

What your parents say to you is similar to what Jesus spoke to His followers— with one major difference. The words of Jesus have eternal impact! In John's gospel, Jesus told those who were following Him what can happen if they both hear His words and believe them. For all who hear and believe Jesus' words will have eternal life. Jesus wants all of us to listen. And Jesus wants us to respond with belief. This faith in Jesus will give us eternal life.

PAUL'S SHIPWRECK

PHARAOH

- The Bible is filled with stories—Abraham, Noah, and others—of people who heard God's Word, believed, and put their faith into action. Rarely was their task easy, but the reward was great. The same will be true for you. Living out your faith will be hard, but Jesus tells us the reward will be amazing—and eternal!

- Pray this prayer: DEAR GOD, I HEAR WHAT JESUS IS TEACHING ME ABOUT ETERNAL LIFE. I BELIEVE! I BELIEVE THAT JESUS DIED ON THE CROSS TO TAKE AWAY MY SIN. PLEASE FORGIVE MY SINS. I PLACE MY FAITH IN JESUS TODAY. THANK YOU FOR GIVING ME THE PROMISE OF ETERNAL LIFE. AMEN.

- This week tell your friends about what Jesus invites us to do—to hear His words and to believe in Him. Then tell your friends about what Jesus promises for all who believe—they receive eternal life! Invite your friends to believe too.

TAKE IT FURTHER

You can read about Noah, a man who heard from God and put his faith into action, in "Rainy Days" in *The Action Bible* or read Genesis 6–7.

BOAZ & RUTH
IN FIELD

WHEN THE STRUGGLE IS REAL

WE ALSO GLORY IN OUR SUFFERINGS, BECAUSE WE KNOW THAT SUFFERING PRODUCES PERSEVERANCE; PERSEVERANCE, CHARACTER; AND CHARACTER, HOPE. AND HOPE DOES NOT PUT US TO SHAME, BECAUSE GOD'S LOVE HAS BEEN POURED OUT INTO OUR HEARTS THROUGH THE HOLY SPIRIT, WHO HAS BEEN GIVEN TO US.

ROMANS 5:3-5

Duncan was thrilled to make it to the championship. Even though the team played hard and the score was close, they lost. After the game, some of the guys cried. The pain of losing the championship hurt deep inside everyone. They all had their sights firmly set on winning. Days later everyone was still in state of mourning. Each teammate suffered in his own way. Their struggle to deal with the loss was real.

The apostle Paul faced many struggles in his life. He suffered for his faith in Jesus. He was even beaten and imprisoned! Yet in his letter to the Romans, Paul encouraged believers to hold on to hope because God was using trials to strengthen their faith.

- It can be hard to realize in the midst of suffering that God is making you stronger and building you up for His purposes. God is producing qualities that will have a powerful impact on your future. It's important to

DANIEL & LIONS

MARY, JOSEPH, & BABY JESUS

188

remember that God does not leave you during those times. If you turn to Him, He will give you hope in the middle of your struggle.

- Here's what you can pray: DEAR GOD, I KNOW I WILL FACE CHALLENGES IN MY LIFE. HELP MY FAITH TO BE STRONG. WHEN THINGS CAUSE ME TO STRUGGLE, EVEN SUFFER, BUILD ME INTO THE PERSON YOU WANT ME TO BE. DEVELOP STRONG CHARACTER IN ME TO PERSEVERE AND NOT GROW WEARY. HELP ME TO ALWAYS FIND MY HOPE IN YOU. AMEN.

- Think of something in your life that has brought you to tears. That was certainly not an experience you'd like to go through again. Now consider the ways God made you stronger because of that difficult experience. Take a few moments to write out three qualities God has developed in you. Tell your parents or a close friend about your growth through the struggle. It will encourage their faith too.

TAKE IT FURTHER

You can read about Paul, a man who faced many challenges and kept his faith, in "Under Arrest" in *The Action Bible* or read Acts 21:17—22:22.

JONAH & FISH

WHEN YOU'RE THANKFUL

I HAVE NOT STOPPED GIVING THANKS FOR YOU, REMEMBERING YOU IN MY PRAYERS. I KEEP ASKING THAT THE GOD OF OUR LORD JESUS CHRIST, THE GLORIOUS FATHER, MAY GIVE YOU THE SPIRIT OF WISDOM AND REVELATION, SO THAT YOU MAY KNOW HIM BETTER.

EPHESIANS 1:16-17

Raul was quickly learning that although he made good money from babysitting his little cousins, it wasn't easy money. He knew his aunt and uncle loved his cousins, but sometimes they seemed so spoiled! They didn't really appreciate their toys and the things Raul did for them when he came over to play. When he got home, it always made him want to try harder to show and tell his parents how thankful he was for what they did for his family.

Gratitude is a way of showing honor to people who make a difference in our lives. It means to show appreciation for and return kindness to others. This is the heart response to the good things people do for us.

The apostle Paul knew that without the kindness and goodness of the Christians in the cities he visited, he would not have been able to continue doing what God had called him to do. He relied on Christians to host him in their homes as he traveled around the world sharing the good news of Jesus.

- We don't say thank you often enough to people for the many good and kind things they do. Have you thanked a teacher for helping you learn

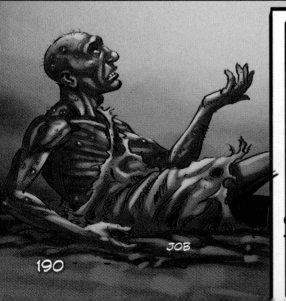

JOB

DISCIPLES IN STORM

math or science? Have you thanked your parents for the food you eat? It's important to pause and say thanks because it shows that you value the difference people make in your life.

- Pause and talk to God: DEAR GOD, THANK YOU FOR THE WONDERFUL THINGS YOU DO! I KNOW ONE OF THE WAYS YOU CARE FOR ME IS THROUGH PEOPLE IN MY LIFE. HELP ME SHOW GRATITUDE TO THEM FOR THEIR SUPPORT. AMEN.

- Think about the people God has placed in your life: parents, teachers, coaches, and friends. These people impact you in many different ways. Stop and thank them for all they do and maybe even write a few thank-you notes this week. They don't have to be fancy but make them sincere. You may be surprised by how your notes make people feel. Be sure to thank God for them, too!

TAKE IT FURTHER

Read one of the many stories of Paul's travels in "Foreign Assignment" in *The Action Bible* and in Acts 11.

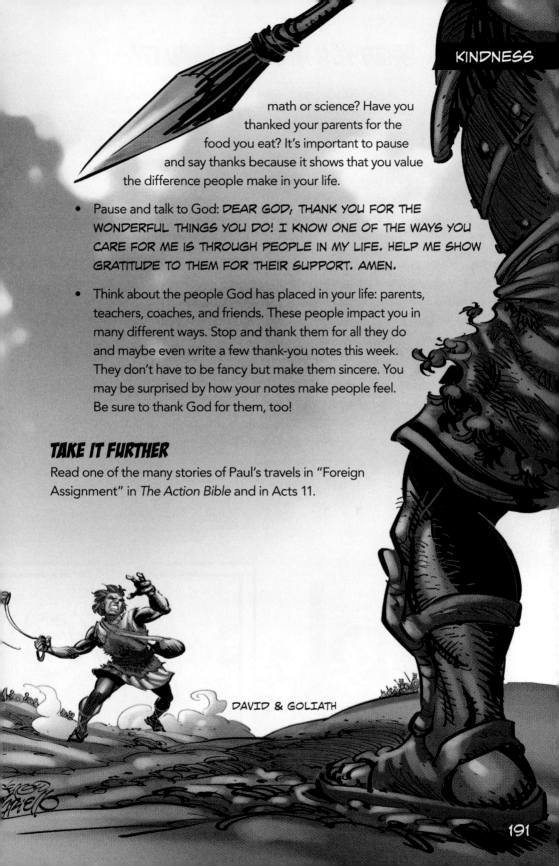

DAVID & GOLIATH

WHEN YOU WANT TO EARN IT!

FOR IT IS BY GRACE YOU HAVE BEEN SAVED, THROUGH FAITH—AND THIS IS NOT FROM YOURSELVES, IT IS THE GIFT OF GOD—NOT BY WORKS, SO THAT NO ONE CAN BOAST.
EPHESIANS 2:8-9

When Avery saw the new bike at the store, she knew she would have to help earn the money to buy it. Her parents gave her some ideas: washing and cleaning her parents' car, picking weeds from neighbors' yards, and walking dogs. Have you ever tried to earn extra money for a special purchase?

In his letter to the church in Ephesus, the apostle Paul said that salvation is very different. It's not something you can earn. No matter what the chore, assignment, task, or job might be, Paul said you cannot *earn* your salvation. It's an amazing gift of God called grace. And because it's a gift that you receive, you can never brag or boast about it. Just receive it!

- Grace is difficult for many of us to understand because it seems like everything in life is about having to work to earn it. In school you earn your grades. In learning to play an instrument you have to practice. In team sports you have to earn the victory. But salvation is different. It's a gift of God for those who place their faith in Jesus Christ. You can't earn it through any good works or achievements.

ANGEL & MARY

MIRIAM

- Close your eyes and talk to God: DEAR GOD, THANK YOU FOR THE GIFT OF GRACE. THANK YOU FOR SALVATION THROUGH FAITH IN JESUS. HELP ME REMEMBER THAT I CAN DO NOTHING TO EARN YOUR APPROVAL, YOUR ACCEPTANCE, OR YOUR LOVE—IT IS A GIFT. YOUR GRACE IS AMAZING! AMEN.

- Make a list of all the different things in your life that you do to earn something—like grades, sports achievements, approval from others, etc. Next, make a list of all the things you do to live a good Christian life. Now, take a colored marker and write the word *Grace* over every word on your lists.

TAKE IT FURTHER

You can read about Jesus' gift of salvation to us in "Crucified!" in *The Action Bible* or continue reading in Ephesians 2.

ESTHER & KING XERXES

WHAT YOUR LEADER NEEDS

I URGE, THEN, FIRST OF ALL, THAT PETITIONS, PRAYERS, INTERCESSION AND THANKSGIVING BE MADE FOR ALL PEOPLE— FOR KINGS AND ALL THOSE IN AUTHORITY; THAT WE MAY LIVE PEACEFUL AND QUIET LIVES IN ALL GODLINESS AND HOLINESS.

1 TIMOTHY 2:1-2

It was the last class of the day, and Georgia was always glad to see her favorite teacher. Ms. Capley cared about making class interesting and helped her become a better student. Today as she walked into the classroom, Georgia could tell something was terribly wrong. As more and more students took their seats and the bell rang, Georgia sent up a quick prayer for Ms. Capley.

Do you pray for those in charge? People like your teachers, church leaders, and coaches? It should be easy to do if you like them and they've had a positive impact on your life. Now consider the principal of your school or the mayor of your city—someone in a position of authority and power you might not know personally but has a lot of responsibility. Do you have someone in mind? The Bible encourages you to pray for that person too! God's people are encouraged to compassionately pray for all people.

In the first letter he wrote to Timothy, the apostle Paul urged his young friend to pray for all people—especially those in positions of authority. Paul wanted Timothy, and all who follow Jesus, to be compassionate toward people. The job

JONATHAN

DISCIPLES

of a leader is hard and stressful. You can ask God to bless them with peaceful lives of godliness.

- As you begin an activity, take a moment to pray for peace and guidance for that leader: teachers at school, coaches at practice, your pastor at church. If you hear other kids speaking harsh words against them, remind them that being a leader isn't easy.

- God hears you when you pray: DEAR GOD, I PRAY FOR THE LEADERS YOU HAVE PLACED IN MY LIFE. PLEASE BLESS THEM WITH PEACEFUL LIVES OF HOLINESS. GIVE THEM THE STRENGTH THEY NEED TO SERVE AND LEAD WITH LOVE. HELP ME TO HAVE TRUE COMPASSION TOWARD THEM. AMEN.

- Once you have prayed for your teacher, your coach, and your pastor, write each person a note to tell him or her that you prayed. Positions of leadership can be challenging. Notes to let leaders know that someone cares for them will be a huge encouragement!

TAKE IT FURTHER

You can read about a challenging time that Moses went through in "The Complaining Begins" in *The Action Bible* or in Exodus 15–17.

MARY, JOSEPH, & JESUS TO EGYPT.

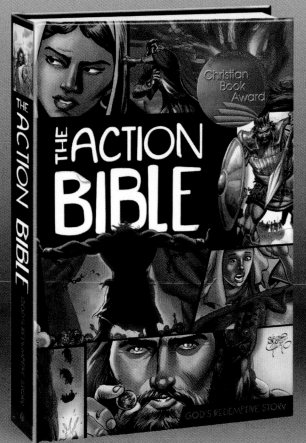

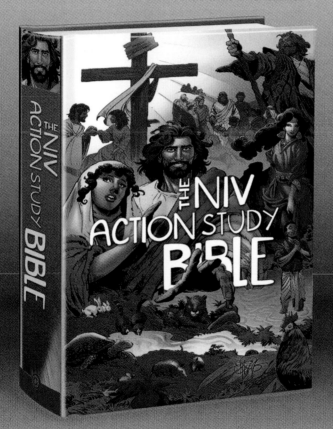